Inside
ARCHITECTURE

Inside
ARCHITECTURE

Stephen Gardiner

A SPECTRUM BOOK

Prentice-Hall, Inc., Englewood Cliffs, New Jersey 07632

Library of Congress Cataloging in Publication Data

Gardiner, Stephen,
    Inside architecture.

    "A Spectrum Book."
    Bibliography: p.
    Includes index.
        1. Architecture—History.   2. Architecture—
Composition, proportion, etc.   I. Title.
NA203.G35   1983   720'.9   83-2484
ISBN 0-13-467381-6
ISBN 0-13-467373-5 (pbk.)

Frontispiece Tile mosaics in the outer portal of the Masjid-i Shah, Isfahan, built 1611–37: brilliant facade architecture of the Safavid period in Persia.

Planned and produced by Equinox (Oxford) Ltd,
Mayfield House, 256 Banbury Road, Oxford OX1 7DH, England
Copyright © Equinox (Oxford) Ltd, 1983

Composition in Palatino by Filmtype Services Ltd,
Scarborough, North Yorkshire
Color Origination by The Siviter Smith Group, Birmingham
Monochrome origination by York House Graphics, Hanwell,
Middlesex
Printed in Italy by New Interlitho, Milan.

This edition © 1983 by Prentice-Hall, Inc., Englewood Cliffs,
New Jersey 07632

A SPECTRUM BOOK

10 9 8 7 6 5 4 3 2 1

ISBN 0-13-467381-6

ISBN 0-13-467373-5 {PBK.}

Prentice-Hall International, Inc., *London*
Prentice-Hall of Australia Pty. Limited, *Sydney*
Prentice-Hall Canada Inc., *Toronto*
Prentice-Hall of India Private Limited, *New Delhi*
Prentice-Hall of Japan, Inc., *Tokyo*
Prentice-Hall of Southeast Asia Pte. Ltd., *Singapore*
Whitehall Books Limited, *Wellington, New Zealand*
Editora Prentice-Hall do Brasil Ltda., *Rio de Janeiro*

Contents

Dedication

This book is dedicated to Michael Scott

Preface

There is often an occasion when we need a guide. If we visit a strange place we may want to know, for example, where the nearest hotel is, and so we ask the way. If we ask a local inhabitant, his directions should be exact and to the point; they will take us there.

An introduction to art should be a bit like a local inhabitant: an informed companion with an intimate knowledge of the subject. But such a guide cannot tell us what conclusions we should come to, what we should feel, or how we should respond. The most we should ask is that it shows us what to look for in art, and helps us to be more observant and more appreciative of art. Personal reactions are the business of individuals. But in helping us to *see* art, the introduction stimulates the imagination; given study, patience and time, this can lead to an increased awareness of the meaning of art.

Like painting and sculpture, architecture is a visual art: buildings are the product of the imagination. Architecture at the present time is much neglected. Many factors have contributed to a breakdown in architectural values, and led to the disappearance of pleasure in architecture as a visual art. The commercial misuse of the machine has reduced buildings to diagrammatic outlines. The lifeline of continuity which has connected styles of the past from as far back as ancient Greek times has been cut by modern architecture. This fact alone would seem to justify this introduction to architecture, the first of its kind.

It is most important that we should be able to look at buildings for ourselves; only by doing so shall we gain the confidence to recognize quality in design and to understand what this quality is. In this respect knowledge can lead to enlightenment, and an enlightened public will lead to better architecture. The disastrous mistakes of the last 25 years have led people to criticize new buildings, yet, while we are becoming aware of what is wrong, unfamiliarity with quality deprives us of knowledge of what would be better, or more fitting.

To bring a coherent pattern to the diversity of architecture, and to make clear its significance and interconnections, this book is divided into 17 chapters, each dealing with an individual style. This is the simplest and, possibly, the only way to avoid confusion; the architecture of towns and cities in different countries otherwise appears as little more than a pile of jumbled pieces from a jigsaw puzzle. An appreciation of styles provides a framework to focus the eye on a particular building or place, and it is part of the purpose of an introduction to do this. We begin, in each case, by explaining the sources of the style – how Gothic structures, for example, were continuations of the Roman arch and vault, or how Georgian residential forms have a starting point in Palladianism. Each chapter then covers the main elements from which architecture is constructed: place, materials, and structure. Each chapter ends by discussing the further development of the style, its spread and international influence.

When we visit a place and notice the spaces which the building enclose, the color and shape of the buildings, we may well like what we see, although we may not necessarily understand why they are arranged or designed as they are. Our curiosity to discover more draws us closer to an understanding of architecture, the elements of which it is constructed, the relationship of one part to another. This process – the way we come upon places and gradually become more involved with them and their detail – determines the plan of this Introduction.

We have selected 17 particular buildings for closer examination because of their great architectural interest, and because they are well known – for example the Pantheon for the Roman style. Here the intention is to assist the reader to form architectural, aesthetic, and technical appreciation of the place selected. We look at the plan of the building, its materials and color, and the multiplicity of detail of which it is constructed. Lastly comes structure, without which no building could be built, but which is often the most hidden part of a building. So we will gradually become aware of a building's significance, and accustomed to the spaces it shapes, encloses, and supports.

Egypt and Early Civilizations

When we think of Egypt we think of pyramids. We picture them as they would have appeared when first built between 4,000 and 5,000 years ago, alone and enormous, out in the desert, an heroic attempt to establish man's presence in a seemingly limitless flat space. Today we see them on the edge of the sprawling suburbs of Cairo; we have to imagine the emptiness that must have once existed.

The pyramid was a tomb. Its form instantly conveys a sense of stability, through clarity of outline and breadth of base, whether as an isolated object or as one element among others. Yet the pyramid was not an Egyptian innovation. The origins of the form began much earlier.

THE ZIGGURATS OF SUMER

The Anu ziggurat (or White Temple) of the Sumerian civilization was built in Mesopotamia from the 4th millennium BC. Possibly inspired by the Sacred Mountain in Mesopotamia (the sloping sides of the main platform suggest this), it was created from a sequence of temples; it was a structure made out of parts. A temple was erected, but when the high priest died he was buried there, and the temple filled in. The Sumerians then built another temple upon it, continuing the process until it was finally topped with the White Temple. Each layer of the ziggurat started life as a temple; the structure of each temple had to be set back from the edge to allow people and processions to

The pyramids of Giza. A heroic attempt to establish man's presence in a world where death was the only certainty

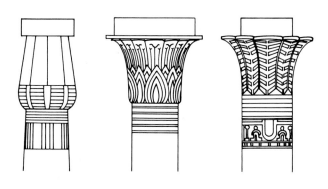

move freely around it. The finished structure was symmetrical and stepped. Other such structures followed; the ziggurat had been born.

Egyptians came into contact with Mesopotamia in the 1st and 2nd Dynasties. Their first pyramid, built at Saqqara by Djoser (ruled 2630–2611 BC), was stepped – probably influenced by the Anu ziggurat. By this time, of course, Anu was a series of solid tombs with a temple at the top; the Egyptians probably adopted its shape without perceiving the principles which lay behind it: they saw a form and a stepped profile, used the style and missed its function. The Step Pyramid at Saqqara was solid. Unlike the ziggurats, its sides were unassailable. Whereas Anu was made of the traditional Sumerian building material – sun-dried mud bricks – Saqqara was stone, increasing security and the solid mass of the structure.

EGYPTIAN ARCHITECTURE

The Step Pyramid at Saqqara was the first pyramid to be constructed in Egypt and the largest in the stepped form. Later the Egyptians simplified the form, stressing its outline and profile. The pyramids at Giza of Cheops, Khephren, and Mycerinus of the 4th Dynasty (2575–2465 BC), and the group of three at Abusir of the 5th Dynasty (2465–2323 BC) are pure geometrical forms. The temple at the top was replaced by a point, and stepped sides became smooth stone. The pyramid was built up layer by layer in steps until the peak was reached and capped, after which the sloping sides were brought down in stone from the top. Structurally, the pyramid comprises four sloping, triangular planes which spring from a square base and meet at a single point; the outline combines with the horizontal lie of the land to complete the shape of the architecture.

Again, symmetrically arranged plans govern the outlines of the pyramid in three dimensions. Disciplines imposed by symmetry are so total that dualities follow in elevation. The eye cannot focus on one of two identical halves placed on either side of a center line. In large groups of buildings such as the Temple of Amon, Karnak, of the 19th Dynasty (1307–1196 BC), the Hatshepsut Temple at Deir el-Bahri

Above: The ziggurat at Uruk, Iraq (Anu ziggurat or White Temple). First steps towards the pyramid form, made by the Sumer civilization

Above left: plant motifs in Egyptian capitals (from left), papyrus bud, closed; papyrus flower; and palm leaves

of the 18th Dynasty (1550–1307 BC), or in the tiny "White Chapel" pavilion of Senwosret I at Karnak of the 12th Dynasty (1991–1783 BC), a succession of symmetrically placed features along the entrance approach determines an axial plan that insists on a precise duality.

The Hypostyle Hall of the Temple of Amon, Karnak. Columns are simple and the plant is stylized as the capital

Temple of Horus, Edfu (3rd century BC). Preoccupation with outlines persists throughout Egyptian culture, from the axial form (as in temple plans) to decorative relief. Above: view from the north. Below: the pylon; hawk god Horus and wall reliefs

The preoccupation with outline, therefore, persists in plan, elevation and form and runs right through Egyptian culture; outlines characterize Egyptian drawings, paintings, sculpture, pottery and reliefs – figures, portrait heads, likenesses of birds, animals and plans are almost always shown in outline and in profile. Similarly with facades of buildings: at the Temple of Ramesses III at Medinet Habu of the 20th Dynasty (1196–1070 BC) great stress is laid on stability through the outlines of inward-sloping ramparts. Columns are simple – see particularly those at Deir el-Bahri and at the Temple of Amon, where the capital is a stylized plant – and entrances are plain – holes framed by stone. The Egyptians showed no interest in perspective; hence the flatness of their designs.

The Egyptian concern with geometry confirmed this flatness of outline. Geometry was important, leading to an exact, secure and stable architecture reflecting the static nature of the Egyptian social structure and civilization. The axial plan of the temple complexes also expresses this stability. The plan of the temple is in three parts, arranged around the axis: the colonnaded courtyard, a hall with its roof supported on pillars (hypostyle) and a sanctuary (although the number of courtyards and halls varied according to the size of the temple). A sequence of experiences follows the axial plan – the ramped entrance, the courtyard open to the sky, the halls roofed with ceilings decorated with stars and lit by clerestory windows. The early experiences – court, main hall – are spacious, but as the way leads deeper into the building, the spaces become smaller, the floor rises, and the ceiling drops in height. The symbolism suggests the path of experience in life which is, after all, modest. The sanctuary is an enclosed cell at the end of the axis, symbolizing the end of life.

Egyptian architecture *was* the pyramid and the temple – the place of eternity and the place of worship. Egyptian energy was almost solely devoted to these two building forms. Death was important; life was not. When a new king came to the throne, he at once selected a site for his tomb and began work on it. The Egyptian use of stone for pyramid and temple, and of mud bricks for all else, emphasizes the distinction between the transience of life on earth and the permanence of life after death. The palace, for example, was not regarded as an important building; it was simply an enlargement of a big house, with a courtyard at the center and a duplication of elements – living rooms, women's apartments, servants' quarters – arranged around an axial plan. No traces remain of palace architecture, except as exact representations in pyramid complexes where everything the Pharaoh knew in his lifetime was reproduced.

Deir el-Medina: Tomb of Pashed (c. 1300 BC). A life recorded for posterity and the after-life in paintings and hieroglyphic writings

THE STEP PYRAMID, SAQQARA

The Step Pyramid of King Djoser at Saqqara, now partly reconstructed, the largest building in the world when it was completed, is one of the most emphatic single architectural statements ever made.

For the Egyptians, its shape and strength must have appeared to satisfy needs bound up with the unknown. It was the belief that life after death was everlasting that led the Egyptian jealously to protect that life, to mummify the Pharaoh's body; and to protect it required a building with a sturdy structure – the stability possessed by the Saqqara pyramid and those that followed.

Everything that Pharaoh used in his lifetime was entombed with him inside the pyramid – treasure that included anything from jewels to chariots, and special offerings from his people on his death. The chamber where his body lay was, therefore, rich in content, and the possessions had to be protected from robbers – a material rather than a spiritual reason for a sturdy form. A house of the dead was attractive to rob because there were few people about to apprehend the thief, and the rewards were good.

Thus the interior planning of the pyramid was, as we see from drawings, exceedingly complicated. It was deliberately designed to stop intruders, by confusing them with a maze of puzzle passages, dead-ends and false directions. The concern for security may also explain the curiously narrow side-entrance to the tomb: the strongly stressed symmetrical approach focused on the pyramid surmounting the temple, which in fact led nowhere. The builders of pyramids went to great lengths to ensure that their dead Pharaoh was safe.

The Step Pyramid, Saqqara

The original flat, then extended and stepped *mastaba* tomb (1-3), was raised in the 27th century BC forming a four-step (4) and finally the existing six-step pyramid (5) encased in Tula marble (6). Below ground a 90-foot shaft (7) descended to the royal burial chamber (8) with galleries leading to the rooms and to the tombs of the pharaoh's family (9-11). Entrance to Djoser's tomb was via a descending passage (12), not the broader secondary shaft (13).

What is known of Egyptian architecture (and this is more in the realms of archaeology than architectural history) perhaps gives an out-of-focus view. What does emerge is continued interest in solid forms and in structures vast in scale, and also the importance of funerary art in Egyptian civilization.

The Pyramids are tombs. They were built to last and built to be seen. It is from the objects buried with the dead kings, in order to assist them in their after-life, that so much is known about the Egyptians. The new use of stone in building was associated with the cult of the dead. In the tomb enclosure of King Djoser (27th century BC) at Saqqara near Memphis, all the buildings were translated from mud-brick and wood into stone. The bundles of papyrus stalks used as supports for the roof of mud-brick buildings were rendered in stone – these ribbed columns later acquired papyrus-styled capitals.

The Step Pyramid of King Djoser was designed by Imhotep as part of an enclosure modeled on that of a palace, a complex of buildings and courtyards, set on a longitudinal axis. The later pyramids at Giza are flat-sided, the Great Pyramid (of Cheops) approached by a gate, a covered passage, a funerary temple and guarded by the Sphinx. The earlier Mesopotamian mud-brick ziggurat with a temple on top expressed yet another idea of reverence for the dead.

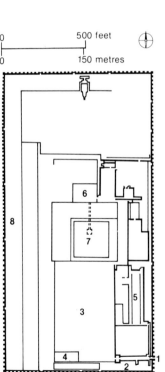

0 ——————— 500 feet
0 ——————— 150 metres

1 Southeast entrance, leading via
2 Colonnade to
3 Great Court, with
4 South tomb
5 Sed festival complex
6 Funerary temple
7 Step Pyramid
8 Enclosure wall

The Saqqara Step Pyramid (*top*) began as a mastaba, then became a four- and then a six-step pyramid, the first in the world. Less than a hundred years later (26th century BC) at Meydum upstream on the Nile an eight-stepped pyramid was converted to a flat-sided one (*center*), but the outer casing fell away. Soon "true" pyramids appeared, designed from the start to be flat-sided. Two of the pyramids at Giza are over twice as tall as the step pyramid at Saqqara. Shown *above* is the pyramid of Sahure at Abusir (5th dynasty, 25th century BC).

The complex viewed from the east — only the 30-foot enclosure wall and the over 200-foot pyramid-tomb itself would be visible.

While the physical function of the pyramid as a tomb was a small, if very important, part of the structure, its gigantic size symbolized the vast influence of the Pharaoh. The aim was a form that had an unequivocal upward thrust toward heaven. But uniquely at Saqqara, the pyramid emerges as a dramatic element in a totally-achieved architectural conception; from the reconstruction, it can be seen that a range of diverse buildings and spaces was resolved in a single composition. The Step Pyramid was designed by Imhotep, who was probably the first architect in history. He was worshiped by the ancient Greeks. His achievements were immense – he was described as "high priest" and "supervisor of everything in this entire land" – establishing him as a god after his death.

The Step Pyramid and the surrounding buildings are enclosed by a 30 ft (9 m) limestone wall making a rectangular area 1,800 ft (550 m) by 900 ft (275 m). The Step Pyramid is placed on the center line of the length of the enclosure and is over 200 ft (60 m) high. Other buildings are planned around several courtyards. The entrance is in the southeast corner and leads into a processional hall at the end of which is a vast court containing the altar at the foot of the pyramid. The Saqqara complex presents a hard, simple form responding to the great flat land of Egypt. Inside, however, the scale drops to the detailed, domestic surroundings of 28 palace structures, colonnades around courtyards and to the more complex planning that arises from everyday living. Both views are dominated by the pyramid, the landmark establishing the order of the conception.

EGYPT, SUMER AND THE INDUS

As we have seen, there were similarities between the architectural styles of the Egyptian and Sumerian civilizations, as there were similarities between the terrain where these civilizations arose; that flat land along river valleys seemed destined to throw up landmarks in the pyramid and ziggurat. There are also likenesses between these landmarks and those of the later Indus civilization (c. 2000 BC) where centers of activity concentrated along the flat plains, near the fertile river Indus. The people of the Indus also adopted the ziggurat, although it is often referred to as a mound.

While Sumerians were preoccupied with relating man to the house, and the Egyptians with creating an everlasting monument, the Indus people were concerned with the relationship of the town with the space outside – the countryside. In their town-planning schemes (at Mohenjo-Daro, for instance, beside the Indus at Sind, and at Harappa, 400 miles to the northeast) they adopted a grid of squares orientated to the points of the compass, linking them with night and day, dark and light. One of the squares in the chessboard was reserved for the mound. It may be a throwback to the Sumerian ziggurat: the top could be reached, and at its peak, as before, was a citadel. From the top it was possible to observe both the town, as it had been created by man, and the countryside. The chief distinction between the ziggurat and the mound lay in a difference of social emphasis; both were the focus of city life, but the mound was related directly to it through the grid plan, and more concerned with the world outside the town.

In enormous plains these landmarks – the pyramid, ziggurat and mound – had to be very large to establish man's position on earth. Egyptian building was, however, by far the largest. The Great Temple of Amon at Karnak covers more space than any other temple in the world, 54,000 sq ft (5,000 sq m). Several of the 134 columns of its Hypostyle Hall are 12 ft (3.7 m) thick and 69 ft (21 m) high (about the size of Trajan's Column in Rome), and are crowned with capitals that could accommodate a hundred standing men. Other columns are 43 ft (13 m) high. Yet this hall was merely the central feature of the entire group of buildings, the area of which would cover much of mid-Manhattan. Within its walls there would be room for St Peter's, Rome, Milan Cathedral, and Notre Dame, Paris. The outer walls could comfortably enclose ten European cathedrals.

The Egyptians wanted a strong structure, and found it in the pyramid. They made it the most stable structure possible before abandoning it. When the pyramids had no further use as tombs (they proved to be failures against the most determined robbers), they continued to inspire men who saw them. Imhotep inspired the Greeks, and gave them the confidence for astonishing achievements.

CHAPTER 2

Ancient Greece

$\mathbf{A}$rchitecture is a product of society. The buildings, and the arrangement of buildings, reflect the nature of society in ancient Greece: freedom, equality, a love of the arts, a passion for theater, a community of people who worked for, and had a share in, the good of the community. Greek architecture describes the spirit of these endeavours: it provided a background order for the diversity of Greek life. Cities such as Delos, Miletus and Priene were laid out on a gridiron plan – an innovation for the Mediterranean. Streets separated a town into orderly blocks of houses which presented only entrance doors and blank walls to the street. Houses, one or two stories high, looked inwards to a courtyard, the focus of home life. But the houses were often very small; life in Greece was a public one and, as in café life today, friends entertained one another at the agora meeting places, which suited the sunny climate. Accordingly, the domestic gridiron plan was always arranged around the public buildings, which provided the focal point.

In architecture and planning the Greeks created a system which, like the laws governing their country, respected both the individual and the community. Aesthetic order was maintained throughout; variations in house types disappeared behind walls, and important architectural statements were reserved for the public buildings – the agora, temples, theaters, assembly halls, educational buildings attached to gymnasia, libraries and so on.

Yet, the theater apart, an aesthetic order was devised which maintained architectural continuity. The Greeks used the peristyle (colonnade) to relate structures with different functions, areas, sizes, and heights; and, in the temples and many secular buildings, they selected a strong, common form for the enclosures behind the peristyle. Both the peristyle and its form were used throughout town centers, with variations of plan, scale and detail. While time has removed the domestic neighborhoods, which now have to be imagined from plans etched in the ground by foundation walls at archaeological sites such as Olynthus (5th century BC) and Pella (4th century BC), many examples of public buildings remain – notably

House of Hermes, Delos. By the 2nd century BC many houses, like this one, were built around a central open courtyard

those on the Acropolis, Athens, and temples and theaters elsewhere. These structures and others, strongly built in marble and stone, have lasted to influence Western architecture for more than 2,000 years.

ORDER AND HUMAN SCALE

Greek public architecture succeeded because it created a background order with a human scale, achieved by the repetition of columns, which framed the view and broke down conventional barriers (walls) that separate the interior of a building from the outside. This introduced the freedom of movement which is important to people, besides relating inside to outside.

We can trace the origins of Greek architecture as far back as 4000 BC, to the hearth, the focus of early houses in Anatolia. Four columns supported the roof around the opening above the hearth; this developed into the characteristic Greek house-plan: the megaron. The

Acropolis: Erechtheum, caryatids. Nearer to human scale than most temples, the figure-columns appear to be in movement, giving a new dimension to structure

structure, with small openings to give a view and currents of air cooling the interior. But the bands of color used remind us of the alternative they did not adopt: these colored lines trace the frame structure.

The Greek temple exploits both solid construction and the structural frame: the megaron enclosure and the peristyle. The enclosure inside had the type of construction and the scale of a domestic roof; but the surrounding peristyle raised this enclosure to a city scale.

The Greeks worked chiefly in stone and marble; there were ample supplies of both. But it was the marble from Mount Pentelicus near Athens, and from the isles of Paros and Naxos, which was of greatest importance to Greek architecture; monumental and strong, it can be cut with exact lines and precise detail. To confirm the marble's durability, this precision survives for us to see today.

THE ACROPOLIS OF ATHENS

The Acropolis stands 512 ft (156 m) above sea level, some 300 ft (90 m) above Athens. Its buildings can be seen from the hills around, standing right above the city, and they can be seen, too, from below, poking up over the rock's fortress wall. Although the Venetians blew up stocks of Turkish gunpowder there in 1687, the Parthenon is not a mere ruin. It remains stunningly beautiful; the entire group of buildings, and their arrangement within a single space, is an architectural masterpiece. The Greeks, while recognizing human failings, believed man could achieve the greatest heights on all sides of life, an optimistic view which is somehow imparted at the Athenian Acropolis. The plan of the Parthenon is direct and immediately comprehensible. The huge Doric columns give a sense of total stability; the plinth supporting them is strong and large, and the structure of the parts which the columns support – the entablatures, the friezes and pediments – is easy to follow. A clear relationship between the different buildings is established by their peristyles so that the view of the columns of one is framed by the columns of the other. The parts are unified with the simplest of means: there is no mystery, no muddle, no confusion. Greek architecture, as represented at the Acropolis, respects the sensibility and intelligence of man. When they were creating the Parthenon, the politician Pericles, the architect Ictinus and the sculptor Phidias had a high view of man. We know this from the friezes illustrating festivals, the gaiety of colors used (no trace of them is left), and the choice of white (as it was then) Pentelic marble, in places washed a honey-color to anticipate the discoloring of time.

hearth was the focus around which all other parts were arranged – living, sleeping, and entrance porch. Eventually a plan developed: a columned entrance porch, an anteroom with a central doorway, a living space (the megaron proper) with a central hearth and four columns supporting the roof around the opening, and a sleeping compartment at the back. On the Greek mainland, houses had pitched roofs – a northern feature – and gable ends. The hearth itself, which also came from the north, gradually disappeared as unnecessary in a hot climate.

The colonnades used throughout the palace of Knossos, Crete (17th and 15th centuries BC), might appear to be the source of the Greek peristyle – Greek use of color in buildings can certainly be traced back to Crete. In fact there are two types of Greek temple structure: one had the traditional oblong megaron form with a gable end to a pitched roof (to throw the water off) constructed of wooden rafters. The second had a peristyle, a frame of columns supporting the entablatures, the friezes and, at the gable ends, the marble or stone pediments. These features can be traced back to Mycenae on the mainland, particularly the Lion Gate and the gateway to the Treasury of Atreus (early 14th century BC). At the Lion Gate, two stone posts supported a lintel, above which stood a triangular relief of two lions. These were standing, indicating the lintel's function of bearing the wall above it. At the gateway of the Treasury of Atreus we find two columns and a flat lintel; the triangular piece of wall is left out as unnecessary. Having discovered the possibilities of post-and-beam construction, the Mycenaeans had a choice of structure: the framed or the solid; for climatic reasons they chose the solid

The Doric Order (above: unfinished temple, Segesta, 5th century BC) supplied the necessary scale to confront the outside world: simple and strong, like natural forms

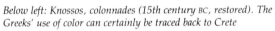

Below left: Knossos, colonnades (15th century BC, restored). The Greeks' use of color can certainly be traced back to Crete

Below right: the Lion Gate, Mycenae (13th century BC). Stone posts and lintel topped by a structurally unnecessary relief

The Parthenon and the Acropolis, Athens

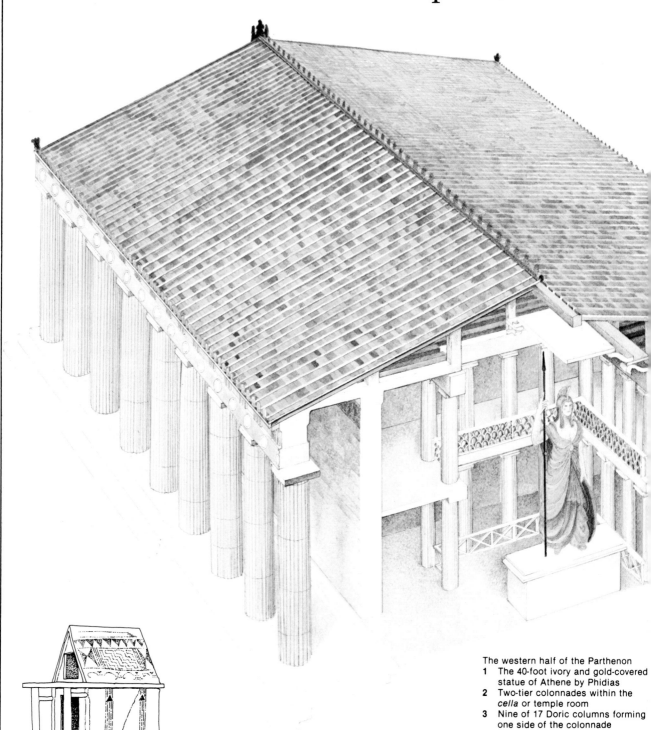

The western half of the Parthenon
1 The 40-foot ivory and gold-covered statue of Athene by Phidias
2 Two-tier colonnades within the *cella* or temple room
3 Nine of 17 Doric columns forming one side of the colonnade
4 The plinth or stereobate
5 Roof timbers
6 Terracotta tile roof
7 The frieze on the *cella* wall
8 Carved metopes alternate with triglyphs above the architrave

There is a connection in western Architecture between early domestic buildings and places of worship. The early Greek houses and the primitive temples shared similar plans and practical details of building. The development of the temple form can be traced from the simple "god-boxes," built in wood (a contemporary model is illustrated, opposite, below), to the refined and developed Parthenon on the Athenian Acropolis.

One important development was the introduction of stone. Originally projecting eaves and colonnades of wooden posts were constructed to protect mud walls. The wooden posts at the porch (indicated in the 9th-century pottery model of a temple illustrated) were extended for the first time to an all-round colonnade at the first temple of Hera on the island of Samos, c. 800 BC. At the temple of Hera at Olympia (c. 600 BC) evidence has been found that its original wooden posts were replaced from the mid-5th century by stone. The different parts of the entablature and pediment of the Parthenon all represent in stone that which was originally made of wood.

In the Athens of the 5th century BC, the Acropolis itself was the place of worship. The Parthenon housed the statue of the goddess Athene, patron of the city, and although it was intended that people should enter to view the statue, the Parthenon was also important as part of a complex of buildings. It was the first large temple to be built of marble and it was conspicuously expensive. Its sculpture retold the Greek

legends of Athene and Athens and the wall of the temple was decorated on the outside with a frieze 524 feet long; there was more exterior sculpture than on any other Greek temple. The subject of the frieze is the Great Panathenaia, the four-yearly procession culminating in the presentation of a new robe to the image of Athene. Beginning down by one of the city gates, the soldiers, horsemen, elders, girls, musicians, and the cattle for sacrifice came up the west slope of the Acropolis and through the Propylaea.

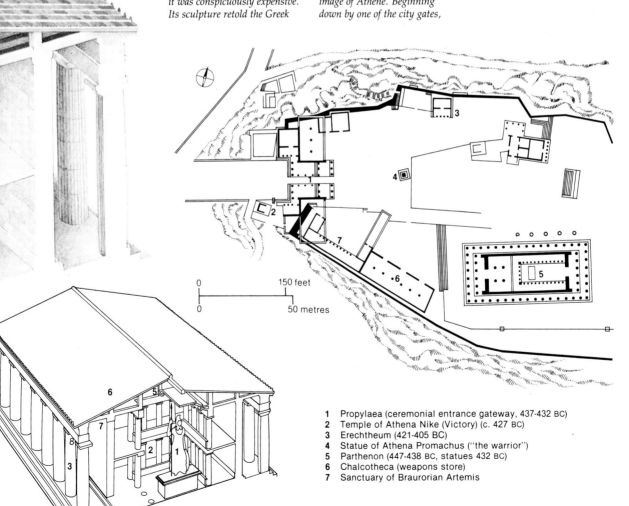

0   150 feet
0   50 metres

1   Propylaea (ceremonial entrance gateway, 437-432 BC)
2   Temple of Athena Nike (Victory) (c. 427 BC)
3   Erechtheum (421-405 BC)
4   Statue of Athena Promachus ("the warrior")
5   Parthenon (447-438 BC, statues 432 BC)
6   Chalcotheca (weapons store)
7   Sanctuary of Braurorian Artemis

But there are also subtle details of design, particularly in the Parthenon itself. Lines of columns, entablatures and pediments appear upright, straight or flat, contributing to the air of calm pervading the Acropolis. Yet there are no absolute verticals in the Parthenon. The columns lean inwards to the extent of nearly 2.5 in (6.36 cm), between top and bottom, and have a slightly convex profile (entasis). The distance between columns varies throughout, because the columns' diameters vary. The spacing of the triglyphs was graded, and, most remarkable of all, the top steps of the plinths and entablatures had an imperceptible curve, based on a radius of 3.5 miles (5.6 km).

The height, width and length of the building, and details such as steps, column diameters and distances between columns, are all governed by the ratio of 4:9.

The inward-leaning columns, entasis and curve were devised to counteract optical illusions and to achieve the greatest possible impression of stability. The buildings on the Acropolis were built by different architects over a period of 40 years (447–406 BC), the Parthenon itself between 447 and 432. Yet they stand together in complete harmony, as though conceived and constructed simultaneously.

In choosing the old megaron form for each building, and in surrounding, or partially surrounding, each building with a peristyle, the architects recognized that their individual work was part of a far larger conception, shown in their extraordinary grasp of architectural scale. For example, the Greeks exploited the immense size of the Parthenon, the largest temple in Greece when it was built, to accommodate the gigantic figure of Athene, by deliberately suppressing the entrance gateway (Propylaea) so that it appears to be part of the rock from which the Parthenon springs. The breathtaking drop in scale between the two buildings vanishes, and the Erectheum (another temple to the worship of Athene) emerges as an ornament for the remaining space.

Scale becomes a matter of detail adjustments. The Parthenon required boldness of form – the Doric column. Inside, the scale drops and we find the lighter, Ionic column. Reflecting the west end of the Parthenon is the Doric portico of the Propylaea: but behind this portico stands the intricacy of Ionic, and the process of scaling down begins. Similarly with the Erectheum; in the southern portico, the scale descends near to human size, columns metamorphose as sculptured female figures (caryatids).

STYLE

The Greek style of architecture which followed the Dark Age – the five centuries of confusion following

Paestum, Italy: Temple of Neptune (c. 450 BC). The traditional oblong megaron form, showing the entrance portico

Acropolis: Temple of Nike. Once inside the Acropolis precinct, the scale drops. The lighter detail of the Ionic column appears

the collapse of Mycenaean civilization – falls into three periods, Archaic (650–480 BC), Classical (480–323 BC) and Hellenistic (323–30 BC). The earlier periods were notable for purity of design, and concern with religious buildings; the Hellenistic, which coincided with Greek overseas expansion, was more decorative, and more concerned with public buildings.

In all periods, the style was composed of parts derived from wood; it has the look of carpentry about it. Early Greek huts and temples were made of columns of tree trunks, diminishing in diameter

Petra, southern Jordan: the Treasury. This late Hellenistic building carved in sandstone still has the characteristic look of carpentry

towards the top, and wood beams – which became the stone entablatures. From early on, columns surrounded the megaron and supported a shallow pitched roof with a gable at the narrower ends. When timber was abandoned for stone or marble, the wood details were copied exactly, particularly in marble, which can be cut with a precision equaling the sharpness of carpentry.

THE CLASSICAL ORDERS

The Greek style was a system of building where structures were made with a repetition of parts. In other words the Greeks selected a part, such as the Doric Order, and, over a long period, perfected it: Doric began as heavy and crude and ended as light and fluted. Having made a good design the Greeks repeated it. There were only three orders – Doric and Ionic in the Archaic and Classical periods (Doric capitals arose directly from woodwork, Ionic from the Egyptian lotus), and the more decorative Corinthian of the Hellenistic period (a variation of the stone Ionic). Nor were the Greeks interested in large spans; when they had to cover a large space, they introduced an additional row of internal columns to subdivide the span.

Doric and Ionic were sufficiently flexible to answer the needs of any situation: Doric supplied the scale to confront the outside world; Ionic was more suitable for the interior. Together they created the frame for Greek architecture and for this reason have gained a somewhat mystical importance.

The influence of Greek architecture for more than 2,000 years has been vast throughout the world: Vitruvius, Alberti, Palladio, and Le Corbusier all returned to it for inspiration. Its parts have traveled widely: we find colonnades, porticoes and pediments everywhere: New York, Helsinki, London, Leningrad, Rome and Sydney. Until the onset of modern architecture, it remained the most popular style in the world.

The Greek Orders

| *Doric* | *Ionic* | *Corinthian* |

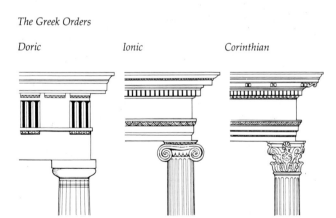

CHAPTER 3

The Roman World

Buildings transmit an impressionistic picture of their age. They help to explain the nature of the society which produces them – what matters most to people, what sort of values they have. The Romans, for instance, addressed themselves to the different kinds of buildings needed to support their highly complex society. If the emphasis in the Greek world was on thought and art, the emphasis in the Roman world was on creative engineering – hence the extraordinary theaters and aqueducts, roads, heating-systems and hot baths. The Romans needed towns and cities that would work for man; their outlook was directed towards good management, discipline, the practicalities of living and the family. Predictably, therefore, they approached their problems in a practical manner: from the beginning they were intelligent collectors of others' ideas.

Below: Pompeii: Casa dei Vetti. The Roman villa was inspired by the atrium house of the Etruscans and by the Greek peristyle

Below right: the Tuscan and Composite Orders of Roman architecture

The Etruscans, great builders who occupied central Italy between 750 BC and 200 BC, and who learned so much from the Greeks, started the Romans off with the arch and the vault, and with their great advances in land-drainage, irrigation and sewer design. The atrium house, with rooms arranged round a pool which collected rain water, was Etruscan; it was the meeting of the atrium and the peristyle of the Greek house (which the Romans also discovered in southern Italy) which produced the tradition of the Roman villa. From the Greeks, too, the Romans adopted the gridiron town plan, with regular blocks of houses arranged round a center of public buildings; they also introduced building lines and controlled building height.

From the Etruscans, the Romans adopted the rectangular temple plan, although for important buildings such as the Temple of Venus and Rome (2nd century AD) they adopted the Greek peristyle form. In the Etruscan plan, the walls to the main rooms were formed of panels between the columns; but the absence of the peristyle broke down the relationship between buildings established by the Greeks.

But the Romans did adopt the column and entablature of Greek architecture for the colonnades of many public buildings – the forum (Roman equivalent of the Greek agora) and basilicas. They also adopted the Greek Orders to which the Etruscans added a simplified version of Doric, the Tuscan Order, and the Romans a development of Corinthian, the very flowery Composite Order. The Romans' single original contribution was a new material: concrete.

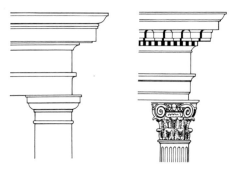

Above: gridiron town planning at Pompeii (Strada dell Abbondganza)

Below: Hadrian's Villa at Tivoli. A concrete copy in Los Angeles houses the collection of another great art collector, J. Paul Getty

ROMAN ENGINEERING

Roman architecture therefore combines Etruscan building and engineering, and the Greek column-and-beam style. In addition to stone and marble quarried in Greece, the Romans made terracotta and brick, and quarried travertine, tufa, peperino, and lava. Their concrete was made of stone or brick rubble, and mortar containing a volcanic earth called pozzolana.

The more ambitious the architectural endeavor, the more the Romans excelled. They developed the Etruscan arch: the Pons Fabricius, Rome (62–21 BC) has a span of 80 ft (24.5 m) and a bridge at Aosta a span of 117 ft (35.5 m). They made a breakthrough in timber engineering from beginnings made by the Greeks; Vitruvius cleared a span of 120 ft (36.5 m) with a triangulated wooden truss at a basilica at Fano, northern Italy. But it was the discovery of concrete which enabled the Romans to cover spaces of a size unequaled until the advent of cast iron in the 19th century. Concrete allowed strong, economic and quick building techniques. It was used as an infill between brick or stone walls, saving skilled labor by allowing masons to concentrate on their craft. Patterns were made in stone or brick tiles, acting as permanent shuttering – superior to the plain concrete finish normally used by 20th-century architects. Concrete was invaluable for vaulting: the stone semicircular barrel vault and cross-vault which the Romans developed were heavy, cumbersome and difficult to build; concrete, poured into shape, suited the curves and awkward junctions which arise in vaulting. From the tunnel of the barrel vault it was not such a long step to the concrete dome built on a circular plan, found in the Pantheon, Rome (AD 120–24).

Concrete also led to the construction of brick and stone piers to reduce waste in walling materials; to coffered ceilings to reduce concrete waste and weight.

Below: Etruscan arch; barrel vault; cross-vault

The Pantheon, Rome

The Pantheon (built AD 120–124) is unique. Most domed circular Roman buildings of the time were small – temples, built in some favored spot, or funerary monuments. Most Roman temples were rectangular with a pediment and portico of columns – of all Roman buildings, the temples were the most conventional. It is in the great palaces, for example Nero's Golden House (begun AD 64), the markets and the baths, that the Romans explored new spatial effects and sequences.

The Pantheon demonstrates the superiority of Roman construction in the way that the arch and concrete are exploited. The building is roofed by a vast dome (wider than that of nearby St Peter's) built out of concrete and buttressed invisibly within the walls, which are of brick with concrete in-fill, and incorporate niches. By using a coffered vault, it was possible to make this a light construction. The coffering was made by constructing a domed brickwork frame, placing wooden "step" shapes in the near-squares so formed and then pouring in the concrete and removing the centering when the cement was hard.

The Emperor Hadrian was a noted builder, and in this temple dedicated to all the Gods (hence the name) which was also a monument to the Empire, the meaning which he intended to give to this work can be read with ease: the dome, the dome of the heavens, the 30-foot wide oculus through which the sun shines, the symbol of the cosmos. Yet in spite of his willingness to explore something new, it is important to understand that Hadrian venerated the past, as is clearly seen in the preservation of the portico (below) where Corinthian columns were part of a temple built in 25 BC. The Roman love of Greek art and architecture is constant.

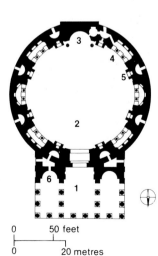

1 Portico
2 Patterned floor
3 Hemicycle niche-buttress
4 Niche
5 One of eight shrines
6 Entrance to staircase to cupola

0   50 feet

0   20 metres

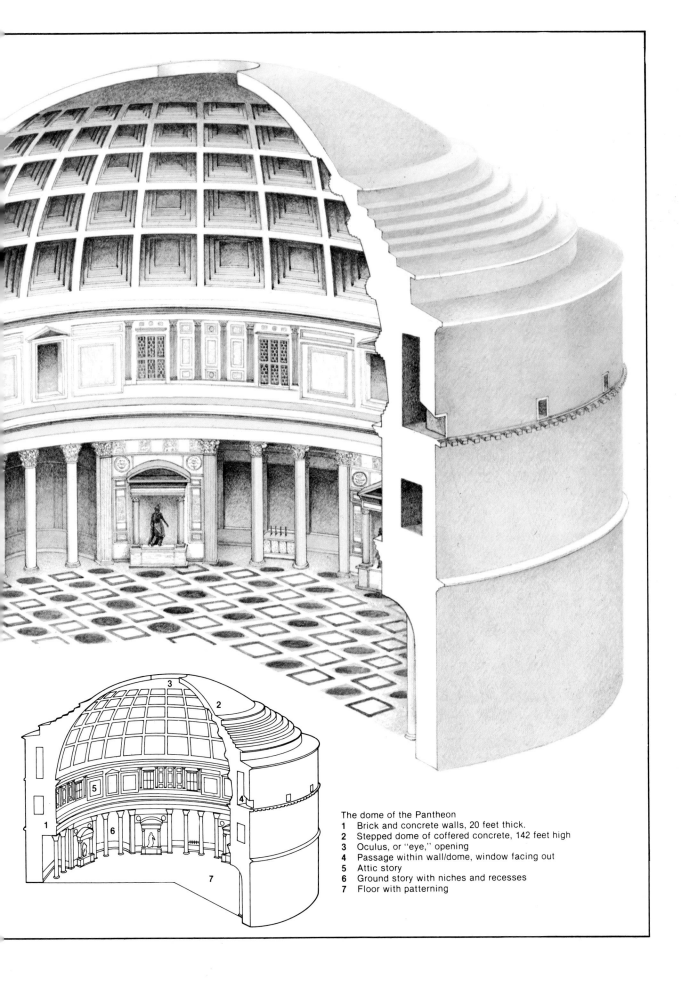

The dome of the Pantheon
1 Brick and concrete walls, 20 feet thick.
2 Stepped dome of coffered concrete, 142 feet high
3 Oculus, or "eye," opening
4 Passage within wall/dome, window facing out
5 Attic story
6 Ground story with niches and recesses
7 Floor with patterning

Pont du Gard, southern France. The greatest achievement of Roman architecture combined with engineering to produce the aqueduct

It resulted in plastered surfaces to cover the roughness of concrete. It made possible aqueducts 100 ft (30 m) high such as the Pont du Gard (AD 14) carrying vital town water-supplies across valleys. The vault and the dome led to the development of the buttress to counter thrusts exerted on walls. The vault, dome and arch, and the concrete which made them possible, led to the dramatic, rich and rounded forms which make Roman building so memorable and distinctive.

THE PANTHEON, ROME

The Pantheon in Rome has a perfect plan: circular with the internal arc of the dome spanning the semicircular space. The building's diameter and height are both 142 ft 6 in (43 m). If you stand in the center immediately below the circular unglazed "eye" in the top of the dome, you have the sense of being in a spherical space.

The echoes of ancient civilizations meet in the Pantheon. From the small piazza outside you see the portico of the megaron jutting out from the drum, reminiscent of the ancient megaron of Greece. The triangular pediment and the curve of the dome complement each other: the frame of columns and the solidity of the drum recall the classical diagram of proportion, where the square is superimposed on the circle. This important theme is followed through in the detail – the circular column on its square base; in the portico floor-patterning, circles and rectangles alternate along the approach path to the building; inside there is a checkerboard of squares and circles. Through such details – the columns and entablatures, the niche and the arch, the repetition of square coffers in the semicircular dome – the architectural conception is majestically completed.

BUILDING THE DOME

The structure of the dome, in coffered concrete, is brought down to the scale of man by the checkerboard marble floor pattern giving us a means by which we can relate ourselves to the scale of the building.

Like the Acropolis, the Pantheon is a story of relationships, but relationships contained within a single space, perfectly conceived and executed, and a simultaneous expression of architectural form and structure. The Pantheon is built up of three tiers, all expressed outside, but inside the dome springs from the top of the second tier. This reduction in the height of the drum has its source in structural, rather than aesthetic, needs: the third tier acts as a huge ring-beam, restraining the forces pushing outwards from the dome. Because the decision on a fundamental matter is made correctly – in the Pantheon arising from the form – subsequent decisions on related matters follow naturally. For instance, the niche opposite the entrance, useful for featuring a piece of sculpture, and as an echo of the semicircular dome, is, in fact, a hemicycle, the name given to the best buttress for retaining earth. The hemicycle was developed in the early days of Roman engineering, and was an important support in the Forum of Trajan (AD 98–113). The niche was one of three types of buttress used at the Pantheon, and occurs at regular intervals round the circumference of the building, forced down by the immense ring-beam. At the Baths of Diocletian (AD 306) and the Basilica of Constantine (AD c. 313) the buttresses are stabilized by heavy statues placed on the top of them, forming pinnacles. The research that went into engineering in the amphitheaters and the aqueducts seems to have found its fulfillment in the Pantheon. As in Classical Greek architecture, no part of its design is superfluous; to remove any single part would cause a structural collapse or an aesthetic failure. The unglazed "eye" in the dome happened because this was the most difficult part to build, yet it brings light to the interior, and a view of the sky. The external shape of the dome had to be flattened at the edge to thicken the concrete ring; but the curve is shallow enough to rhyme with the pitch of the pediments. The concrete had to be stepped for additional strength, but the lines of the steps stress the circular form of the dome. The Pantheon is to Roman architecture what the Parthenon is to Greek; its influence on the Western world was similarly immense.

SPREAD OF ROMAN ARCHITECTURE

The round form in the rotunda, the arch, the dome, the barrel vault and the niche was central to the Roman forms, and, in structural terms, the strongest. The Pantheon and the oval Colosseum (AD 68–100) were immensely strong, so that they have lasted where other buildings have not. They were strengthened by the cavity between the outer and inner skins of the brick walls (at the Pantheon) and stone walls (at the Colosseum) filled with concrete.

The sphere uses the minimum surface area to cover a given space. The Romans realized that if design conflicts with certain natural laws, the structure will fail. The Romans not only recognized these laws, but used them as a springboard for their creative ideas. No wonder, then, that the Roman style is remembered for the stupendous arches of the Pont du Gard rather than for rectangular temples, and for the double-story vaults of the Basilica of Constantine rather than for colonnades of fluted columns. With the Romans, architecture moved into the area of creative structure for the first time. The Romans developed confidence to build hot baths, palaces, basilicas, and theaters, all remarkable for boldness of plan and ambitious structure.

The Roman style spread as the Roman empire expanded. Wherever the Romans settled, their entire equipment for living followed – the gridiron town plan, aqueducts, temples, basilicas, houses, hot baths, theaters, bridges, and tombs. Roman technology was so advanced that its progress was irresistible: a villa in England or an aqueduct in Spain was still a Roman villa or a Roman aqueduct – it gained little from the indigenous style. And so Roman buildings, or their

Colosseum, Rome. One of the many huge structures made possible by concrete, which here filled the cavity stone walls

remains, are found all over Europe and around the Mediterranean – in England, France, Spain, Germany, Greece, Lebanon, Syria, and North Africa. The Pantheon itself strongly influenced particular buildings of Andrea Palladio, but Roman influence also recurs in various other styles; in buttresses, vaults and in the gridiron town plans which swept modern North America.

Rome: Basilica of Constantine. When the Romans discovered the arch, all was arches, vaults and domes

Baths of Caracalla, Rome (3rd century): mosaic. The discovery of concrete saved skilled labor, and craftsmanship flourished

CHAPTER 4

Byzantium

The Byzantine style of architecture brought together the square plan of the Greek cross and the dome of the Roman world; the result has curious echoes of the domed, mud-brick houses of Khirokitia.

The Emperor Constantine recognized Christianity as an official religion early in the 4th century. Architecture now began to center on the church. The cross makes rare appearances in early Christian art, but never decisively until Byzantine architecture, where it celebrates the new freedom to practice Christianity. Byzantine architects found a strong architectural form in the symbol of the cross, which provided the foundation of their style. The Greek cross, as this form has come to be called, also provided the church with a covered space in which people could gather for worship: a plan focusing on the center crowned with a dome – contrasting (although some basilicas were still built) with the normal early Christian basilica, with its processional nave and aisles. To create the style the Byzantine architect discovered a method of supporting a round dome on a square base. The Roman dome had been built on a circular drum, a comparatively simple problem to solve. The Syrians attempted to solve the new problem by laying triangular slabs at the corners, turning the square into an octagon; however from below the view of triangular pieces of stone conflicted with the circular form. At the octagonal Mausoleum at Spalato, Dalmatia (AD 300) the Romans made a late breakthrough in brick vaulting; three brick arches projected to meet the triangular stone, covering and concealing it in a method known as the squinch. Yet it was still something of a compromise: the plane of the last arch's wall still conflicted with the circular form.

The complete solution to the problem had to wait for the construction of Santa Sophia, Istanbul, where convex-curved corners called pendentives made the transition between the square base and the dome's circular base.

A further development appears after the 11th century; the dome is raised on a drum above the pendentives; from this centerpiece the plan branched out as a Greek cross, the barrel vaults over the arms of the cross carrying the thrust from the dome. Raising

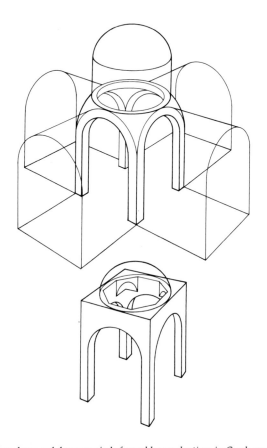

Top: dome and drum on circle formed by pendentives in Greek-cross plan. Bottom: dome on octagon formed by squinches

the dome on a drum stressed the intersection, symbolizing the point where, on the cross, the mind and body came together in the heart. The Byzantine architects' determination to pursue the symbolism of the cross, and the artistic purity of their interpretation, showed the strength of their faith.

Plan of a basilica: S. Apollinare in Classe, Ravenna

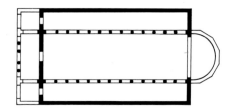

THE BYZANTINE DOMED TOWER

The dome, the drum and the Greek cross are the principle elements in Byzantine church architecture. The spaces left by the cross at the corners were enclosed with four further compartments, echoing the corners of the square base to the dome that were filled by four pendentives, while the curved vaults covering the four arms of the cross were covered with pitched roofs, and the pendentives built up to make a square base. The church of Kapnikarea, Athens (1060–70), follows this pattern. At St Irene, Istanbul (remodeled 740), the interior vault on the southeast side is visible as a line immediately below the gable end of the pitched roof, while, internally, the curved pendentives appear at the corners of the central space below the dome. The drum supporting the dome was sometimes octagonal; on these occasions the Byzantine builders reverted to the Roman squinch. The octagon was constructed of a series of large arches; to achieve a satisfying transition from octagon to dome, small pendentives were introduced between the arches to complete the circle on which the dome was carried,

The combined effect of the tall, slender domed tower and the square body of the church below made the Byzantine church a strong form. In principle, the pattern is the same whether at the huge cathedral of Santa Sophia or at a tiny church such as Kapnikarea. Yet the detail was as complex as it was festive. The central dome was covered with Roman tiles laid to follow the dome's arc, sometimes the edge of the dome was horizontal, sometimes it curved over the arches of windows in the drum or tower like eyebrows. Sometimes the central dome was surrounded by groups of smaller domes of various heights over the arms of the cross or over the corner compartments.

No good building stone was available in Constantinople; the best use had to be made of available materials – largely clay for bricks, rubble for concrete; marble and monolithic columns had to be imported from quarries along the shores of the Mediterranean. Limited materials were used in the richest and most decorative manner possible. Thick layers of mortar were laid between brick tiles about 1.5 in (4 cm) thick and stone blocks. Tiles and stones were laid in alternate bands, or tiles were arranged in different patterns, the stones laid with strict regularity. Corbels were used for sculptural friezes under roofs, and friezes continued as thin circular brick ribs beside windows and over arches. Stonework was carved with intricate pictures and patterns, for example at the Small Metropolis, Athens (c. 1250). These details fused to turn works of architecture into gigantic and sublime pieces of sculpture.

Above: Antiphonitis church of the Blessed Virgin, Ayios Ambrosios, Cyprus (12th century) and (below) St Nicholas, Rhodes (13th century)

SANTA SOPHIA, ISTANBUL

Santa Sophia, Istanbul, was completed in 537. It was designed for the Emperor Justinian by two Greek architects, Anthemius of Tralles and Isidore of Miletus, and unbelievably took only five years to build. It is the supreme achievement of Byzantine architecture; it was huge, but magnificently simple in its conception. Although the structure was most complex, all the parts were so faultlessly related that what finally emerged was a single object. Santa Sophia was one of the first religious buildings where the Greek cross shows clearly in the plan. The plan dictates the structure; the pendentive was discovered at Santa Sophia.

Santa Sophia, Istanbul

Justinian's great cathedral was both the emperor's private chapel and the great cathedral of Constantinople, the largest church in Christendom. The central plan was traditional for private chapels at this time, but Santa Sophia had also to accommodate a large congregation. The east (or southeast) end was the holy of holies for the patriarchs, the emperor and his cortege were permitted in the main space, others were only allowed in the aisles and the women in the galleries. These different needs were met in the centralized plan (top right) of a Greek cross within a square. The plan of the architects Anthemius of Thralles and Isidore of Miletus focused on the huge dome, 107 feet in diameter. The engineering was exceedingly daring, and the dome fell down shortly after Justinian's death in 565. Originally semi-elliptical in section, it was rebuilt as a hemisphere, as this form exerts less thrust on the walls. The external buttresses are also later, and the minarets, added by Turkish conquerors in the 15th century.

Raising a dome was a complicated structural problem. Methods were developed to bridge the change of form from square base to circular dome – the squinch and the pendentive, the latter perfected in Santa Sophia. In addition to the four great piers, a descending series of domes, semi-domes and hemicycle niches distrubuted the thrust of the brick dome to the ground (see the north-west–southeast section, far right).

Little of the original riches of marble and mosaic decoration survive. The icon-like mosaic portrait of Emperor Alexius I Comnenus (below) from the south gallery dates from the 11th century.

1 Pier
2 Pendentive
3 Dome
4 Semi-dome
5 Hemicycle
6 Oval nave
7 Gallery

0   100 feet

0   40   metres

Above: Santa Sophia. The Greek cross plan made the central space the focus where the faithful could gather as one body

Below: mosaic of paradise, S. Apollinare in Classe, Ravenna

The Greek cross was vast; the central dome covers an area of 9,000 sq ft (840 sq m), and is raised on pendentives 180 ft (55 m) above the square floor. The Greek cross plan had to be adjusted to support the enormous loads transmitted from the center, a problem that was resolved within a system of domes and semi-domes, contained within the overall near-square plan. The northeast and southwest arms of the cross ended in huge hemicycles (the buttress which the Romans had developed and used with great effect at the Pantheon as a niche) covered with semi-domes; the space enclosed by the hemicycles and semi-domes forms an enormous oval nave, 220 ft (67 m) long and 107 ft (32.5 m) wide. These hemicycle buttresses were immensely strong; but on the northern and southern sides stand eight further vast buttresses each 25 ft (7.5 m) wide and 60 ft (18 m) long. Between them the hemicycles and buttresses gradually lower the loads from the center, stepping down, roof by roof, dome by semi-dome, until the safety of the ground is reached. Inside, this sequence of domes and semi-domes appears to be a single dome of fantastic dimensions constructed of separate pieces. At the same time, this succession of domes and semi-domes reduces the scale from the lofty center by a gradation of parts to the two-story arcades along the aisles. They are covered with a surface sheeting of marble – Phrygian white, Laconian green, Libyan blue and Celtic black among others.

Thus the interior has a richness of detail that naturally evolves from structural forms – the dome was both the roof-form and the interior ceiling shell. In this, the major religious building built by the Byzantines, the architects originated a form of dome construction which, scaled down, suited town and village churches too. When you go to a small church and find the Greek cross, and look up and see that the dome is supported on pendentives, it is extraordinary to think that this was made possible by the architects of Santa Sophia, and has remained practically unchanged throughout the lifetime of the Byzantine style.

INFLUENCE OF BYZANTIUM

The Greek cross and the pendentive were the major contributions of the Byzantine style: the two had an immense influence on the architecture of Europe. Santa Sophia was copied in the Mosque of Sultan Ahmed (the Blue Mosque), Istanbul, in 1616. Modified to accommodate Western processional requirements, the Greek cross was adopted for Gothic church and cathedral plans; with an elongated nave it became the Latin cross; Ravenna, Italy, the seat of representatives of Byzantine emperors, was a center of Byzantine architecture; S. Vitale, Ravenna (c. 532–47), with a

Marble, mosaic, and carving at Aachen, Charlemagne's chapel based on S. Vitale, Ravenna. Here the dome was raised up on a drum, in this case octagonal, to achieve a satisfactory transition internally and a stronger form externally

At St Mark's, as at Santa Sophia, pendentives connected the square space with the dome above. The building brought the Byzantine style to Venice in the 11th century. The Greek-cross plan is surmounted by the domes, the largest in the center (see below)

dome on its octagonal form, was copied by Charlemagne at Aachen in the Palatine Chapel (792–805). In Venice, closely linked with Constantinople by trade, the Greek cross, surmounted by five domes (the largest at the center of the cross, with a dome for each arm), dominates the form of St Mark's (1063–85). This building was very influential; it brought the Byzantine style to Venice as a whole. The influence of detailed decoration, as on the outside of the Doge's Palace (begun 9th century), led on to the Italian Renaissance. Finally there is the characteristic Byzantine window – with a central column supporting the meeting-point of two little arches. When we think of the Byzantine style, it is this detail, as much as any other, that comes to mind and which reappears so often abroad – as arcades at the 11th-century S. Fosca on Torcello near Venice for example, or as balcony facades in 15th-century Venetian palaces. While there is a perfect Greek cross with five equal domes in a close copy of St Mark's in the church of St-Front, Périgueux, France (1120), Byzantine windows can be found even further away, and in another style, at La Madeleine at Vézelay.

CHAPTER 5

Islam

One of the strangest experiences a traveler can have is to stumble upon the Great Mosque in Córdoba, Spain. He might well wonder for a moment whether he had taken the wrong plane and arrived at the Taj Mahal, Isfahan, or even Mecca. One of the astonishing facts about Islamic architecture is the distance it traveled in less than 80 years. When the prophet Muhammad died in AD 632, the new religious movement proclaimed by him spread from the Arabian peninsula to Turkey in the north, India in the east, and to the Atlantic coast of North Africa and to Spain in the west. Islamic architecture was a product of this religious movement; the distances traveled by the architectural style, and the consistency of its appearance from one continent to another, are proof of the strength of the Islamic faith.

Islam centered on God, and on the mosque; the design of the mosque influenced the buildings around it, whether religious or not. Two essential characteristics determine the style: first, exceedingly intricate,

Córdoba: Great Mosque (10th century). The striped horseshoe arches vanish into infinity like striped canvas awnings covering a market. The mosque was originally a vast religious bazaar

exotic patterns in watery, brilliant colors covering the facades and domes of the mosques. Arabia had no distinctive architectural traditions; the genius of the Islamic style must have been inherited from countries with such traditions – Syria and Lebanon, parts of the Byzantine empire until the Muslims overran them in the early 7th century. These countries were rich in building materials, in particular, clay for brick-making, various marbles, lime for mortar, and plaster; they also boasted a long tradition of ceramics, gypsum plaster, glass, and metalwork. Persia, overrun a decade or so later, had an old tradition of carpetmaking. The dense patterns, often derived from flowers, roots and ancient scripts (the Muslim faith forbade any representation of the human figure) were transferred to mosques, whose facades often seem indistinguishable from carpets; the flat facades are the second distinctive characteristic of the Islamic style.

THE COLOR OF ISLAMIC ARCHITECTURE

Possibly the absence of a deep-rooted architectural tradition in the country which gave birth to Islam accounts for a certain unreality which pervades the style; from traditions picked up from different countries evolved an architecture with a missing central piece, resulting in a nomadic, temporary air. But the bright colors accompanying the style suit the climates of the countries to which it traveled – Syria, Egypt, North Africa, Iran, and Spain with their dry, clear climates. The brilliance of Persian colors seems to be a celebration of the wonderful discovery of water in a desert. Water means life: Persian color describes life in the carpets, textiles, clothes, paintings, and buildings. In particular, the carpets seem inspired by the channeling of water in formal patterns, leading to, and among, the intricate roots of trees and flowers. Certainly the combination of shining ceramic mosaic (blue was the favorite Persian color) and clear running water has a supernatural irridescence.

In Islamic buildings, the structure was put up in simple and traditional ways, to receive the multi-colored cladding. There were no structural innovations. There are traces of Roman and Byzantine

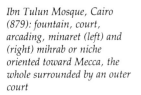

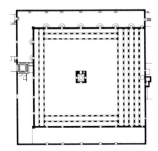

Ibn Tulun Mosque, Cairo (879): fountain, court, arcading, minaret (left) and (right) mihrab or niche oriented toward Mecca, the whole surrounded by an outer court

The Taj Mahal, Agra (17th century). Within the platform the Turkish Mogul architect employed pools of water to achieve the perfect reflection of absolute symmetry

Above: Samarra, Iraq, dome with carpet-like cladding and, beyond, the minaret of the Great Mosque (9th century). Right: the Great Mosque, Isfahan (11th century). Blue was Persians' favorite color

influence in barrel-vaulting and cross-vaults in small spans; but large flat or pitched roofs were constructed of timber – for example, at the Great Mosque in Damascus (705–15).

Dome structures followed Byzantine principles of pendentives, which were developed on a larger scale than at Santa Sophia when this building was copied in the Blue Mosque, Istanbul (1616). The Blue Mosque

The Alhambra, Granada

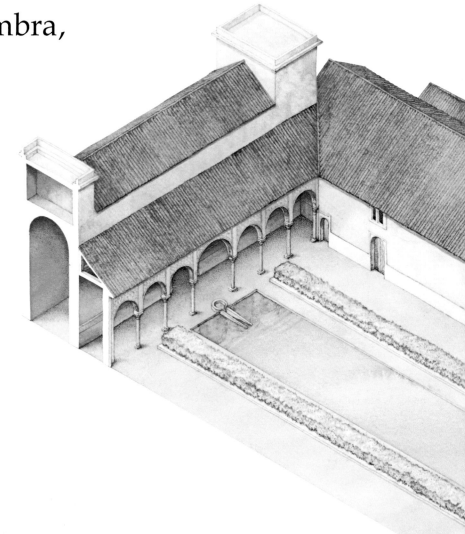

The "Moorish" style of Islamic architecture evolved in Spain, where the traditions brought by refugees from Damascus met those of the Visigoths. The beginning of the Great Mosque at Córdoba in the 8th century was an important step in this development.

The Alhambra, in Granada, is secular, a palace with a small mosque as part of the palace complex contained within the walls of the citadel. Built in the 13th and 14th centuries, it was the residence of the last Moorish kings in Spain, the Nasrid Kingdom of Granada. The Palace must have appeared very different originally, before the damage caused by the Christians, victorious in 1492, and more recent restoration. For instance, the Hall of the Ambassadors, once the throne room, had all its stucco brilliantly colored and gilded and the windows filled with stained glass set in plaster.

Glazed tiles, pierced stone, marble columns and carved plaster (including "honeycomb" and "stalactite" work) in profusion attest to the highly developed decorative skills of the craftsmen. The arcading and gabled portico that overlook the bronze lions bearing an alabaster basin (right) belong to the Court of the Lions, the king's private patio.

The interest in decorative form extends beyond the treatment of the surface with patterns, quotations from the Koran, and pierced stone work, to a reduction of the architecture and to a lack of all interest in expressing structure. Architectural forms are reduced in force, the single arch, a strong axial feature, is reduced to two arches and becomes therefore a decorative motif. The vault of the Hall of the Abenceragas (south terminal of the north-south axis) is covered in carved stucco. These plaster "squinches" turn the square into an eight-pointed star, the star is then extended into a drum, which is closed by a dome again covered in stucco "squinches." But the entire vault is made from plaster and suspended from a concealed wooden frame. The squinch form, originally a structural method for turning a square into the circular base for a dome, is thus transformed into a purely decorative feature.

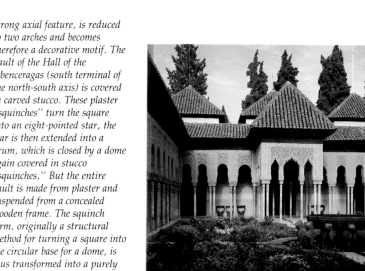

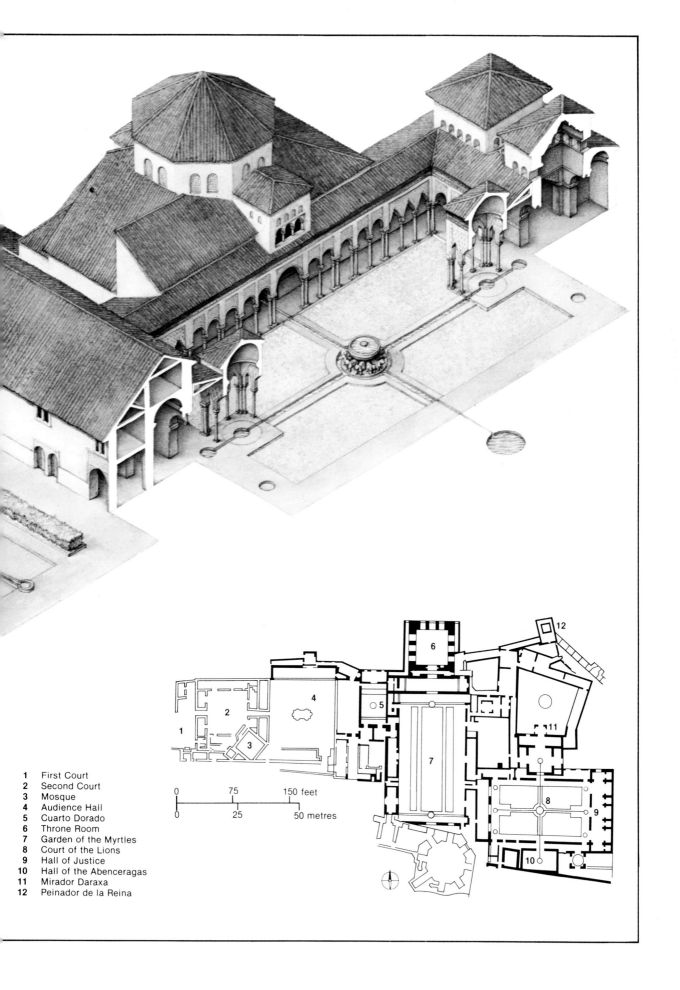

1 First Court
2 Second Court
3 Mosque
4 Audience Hall
5 Cuarto Dorado
6 Throne Room
7 Garden of the Myrtles
8 Court of the Lions
9 Hall of Justice
10 Hall of the Abenceragas
11 Mirador Daraxa
12 Peinador de la Reina

0   75   150 feet
0   25   50 metres

Damascus: Great Mosque. Islamic builders were less interested in Roman and Byzantine architectural discoveries than facade decoration. Large flat or pitched roofs were still constructed of timber

was provided with as big a space as possible, to bring together under one roof an enormous crowd of the faithful. Instead of separating the side spaces, as at Santa Sophia, at the Blue Mosque the structure was arranged to draw together all the people in one space. The architect of the Blue Mosque, Sinan, first perfected

Istanbul: Blue Mosque. As large a space as possible was provided here by the architect Sinan. The plan was inspired by Santa Sophia, but simpler in conception

this kind of symmetrical mosque, with one enormous dome on pendentives flanked by four semi-domes, at the Mosque of Selim II or Selimiye Cami, Edirne (1569–75). At the Blue Mosque, as at Santa Sophia, the exterior form exactly mirrors the interior space, although the former was simpler in conception, and structurally more advanced, than the Byzantine building to which it owed its inspiration.

THE ALHAMBRA, GRANADA

Spain, at the western end of the Islamic empire, harbored numbers of Syrian refugees who fled there to escape death. The Palace of the Alhambra, Granada (1338–90), a direct result of the Syrian immigrants' presence, is one of the finest Islamic architectural works.

There are two palaces at Granada. The most important is the Alhambra; across the ravine to the east is the Generalife, the country palace, with its gardens. The Alhambra itself is a fortified palace on the top of a hill immediately overlooking the city, surrounded by vast ramparts (begun in the 13th century by Muhammad ben Alhamar) behind which stood a collection of buildings separated by courtyard gardens, including a mosque and its ancillary buildings. These were arranged around a courtyard which led into an open audience space separating the mosque from the palace itself.

Today only the palace remains, its composition focusing on two exquisite rectangular courtyards; the Garden of the Myrtles, 130 ft × 75 ft (39.5 m × 23 m), for public ceremonies is slightly larger than the Court of the Lions, 115 ft × 66 ft (35 m × 20 m), the monarch's private garden courtyard. Each has a different character, suiting its different function. The Garden of the Myrtles is open and light, its spaciousness heightened by a large, symmetrically-placed reflecting pool. In contrast, the Court of the Lions breathes a secret, sacred atmosphere, shrouded on all four sides with arcades like curtains; there is no reflecting pool, merely channels of fast-running water leading to a central fountain of lions. In the Garden of the Myrtles, delicate with the scent of jasmine, roses, honeysuckle and myrtle leaves, the sun reaches every corner of the sharp white marble floor at some time of the day; in the Court of the Lions, however, the perforated alabaster arches allow only filtered glimpses of sun.

Halls and ancillary rooms adjoining the two courts match the differing characters of each. The Hall of the Ambassadors (containing the Throne Room) in the huge Tower of Comares at the north end of the Court of the Myrtles, is a simple cubic chamber crowned by a polygonal dome. The Court of the Lions, on the other

Jerusalem: Dome of the Rock. Only the strong building form transcends this degree of decoration (much restored). Below the wood-framed dome is an octagonal ambulatory

hand, terminates at its east end with the highly complex detail of the elaborate Hall of Justice. The contrasting atmospheres of the two courtyards is one of the most memorable features at the Alhambra.

The chief architectural fascination of these courtyards, as with those in the Generalife, is the way the space of the entire building is conveyed: by sunlight penetrating traceried arcades, by the brightly patterned surfaces, and by the sound of trickling water from fountains. This consciousness through light, shadow, color and sounds leads to a unity of space; the Alhambra was constructed from details of bewildering complexity.

The structure of the Alhambra was disguised by fantastic decoration; but however flimsy it appears, it was better constructed than most Islamic architecture, thanks to the knowledge of contemporary Gothic engineering. Nevertheless, the Alhambra, like so much other Islamic architecture, is a collection of pieces which, although like the Court of the Myrtles often perfect in themselves, remain unrelated. Coherent architectural conceptions of the kind found in the Golden Mosque, Baghdad and, to a lesser degree, in the Blue Mosque, Istanbul, are rare indeed.

INFLUENCE OF THE STYLE

The Islamic style was unique; it had little connection with any style which preceded it, was currently evolving, or which followed. It is a direct result of Islamic metaphysics. The only matter of real importance is contemplation of the soul: reality and substance existed within – everything external was reduced to diagrams and symbols: The architecture is two-dimensional, flattened by pattern, and arranged like pages of a scrapbook.

Religious building was reduced to a structural framework filled with color and pattern. The facades, both inside and outside, became the canvases on which the artist worked, contrasting with the West, where the walls of contemporary church buildings were used for frescoes and mosaic decorations. In Islamic architecture, the importance of the structure – of walls, columns and roofs – was suppressed by corner-to-corner, eaves-to-ground decorative cladding. This was an expression both of indigenous Persian textile and carpet design and of the dry climate; little rain meant that traditional methods of throwing off water, which can lead to complex moldings and entablatures, could be discarded. In Islamic mosque architecture shapes are simplified to the edge of pointillist art, and only the strongest building forms transcend decoration: for example the domes, the chambers of prayer, the arcaded courtyards that we see at the Dome of the Rock, Jerusalem (690–92), the Shrine of Mashhad, the Golden Mosque of Baghdad, and the Tomb of Rukn-i 'Ālam at Multan, Pakistan (1320–24).

Characteristics of the mosque style passed to other buildings. In palaces the garden is possibly the most important element in the schematic design; there the decorative facades relate the building to the natural world of color around it. The architecture that we find in different countries, continents and centuries has a remarkable similarity, just as pottery, metalwork, and leather design did. Islamic art remained faithful to Mecca. It was orientated, as the mosques were physically through the alignment of their axes, towards the heart of the Islamic world. The style was so focused that it did not develop, but always returned to its starting point.

CHAPTER 6

Middle America

Visitors to Middle America are often baffled by what they find there: isolated ziggurats on level stretches of bare ground; huge mounds of stone with terraced sides and flat tops; enormous flights of steps making for the sky and emptiness, or for some singularly dignified windowless ruin; stumps of broken-off columns; massive standing figures like fossilized gods; missing climaxes to missing vistas.

You clamber up the Pyramid of the Moon at Teotihuacán, 30 miles from Mexico City, and look across the traces of some kind of geometric architectural plan towards the Pyramid of the Sun. You wonder when it was built, what it originally looked like, what it all meant. There is not much to go on; this great civilization was destroyed about AD 800, and almost every vestige had disappeared by the 16th

Above: Plaza, Monte Albán. The terracing of the mountainsides for cultivation was reflected in such groups of pyramids

Below left: Tula. These stone caryatid columns on top of a pyramid originally supported the roof a temple (7th-9th centuries)

century, when Cortés arrived in 1519. All that is left of a thousand years of art and architecture are lumps of brick and stone in abandoned structures.

The scale and detail of the pyramids makes us aware of the greatness of the civilization. Many related civilizations existed in Middle America, notably Mayan (3rd century BC–AD 1528), Teotihuacán (150 BC–AD 750), and Aztec (AD 1325–1519). Agriculture, particularly maize cultivation, was vital, and depended on the right weather. Concern with nature's forces showed in architecture; superstitions, fears, and gratitude could be expressed permanently through buildings. Most important for these people were the sun, moon, rain and corn gods, natural phenomena crucial to survival. For the Aztecs and their predecessors Tlaloc presided over rain, agriculture was represented by Centeotl, Tezcatlipoca was god of good fortune and chance, but also appeared as the four compass points, and as "the seasons." The duality of life was displayed by Ometecuhtli and his wife, Omecihuatl, the creator-gods.

THE SIGNIFICANCE OF THE ZIGGURAT

The ziggurat surmounted by a temple was the most important building type. The terracing of its sides, recalling the Sumerian ziggurat of Mesopotamia (similarly surmounted by a temple) may have been inspired by the terracing of mountain sides to help cultivation (the wheel had not been invented) and restrain the precious earth. The temple at the top séing as the house of god was a relatively small structure, deriving from the house form. High up on the ziggurat, it provided an architectural focus for the spiritual and everyday life of the city, like the

Above: El Tajín, Pyramid of the Niches. The pyramid exterior was used, unlike its Egyptian counterpart, in the ritual ascent

Below: Chichén Itzá, El Castillo. Stepped, with a flat top for the house of God: a man-made sacred mountain, like those of the Indus

The Pyramid of the Moon, Teotihuacán

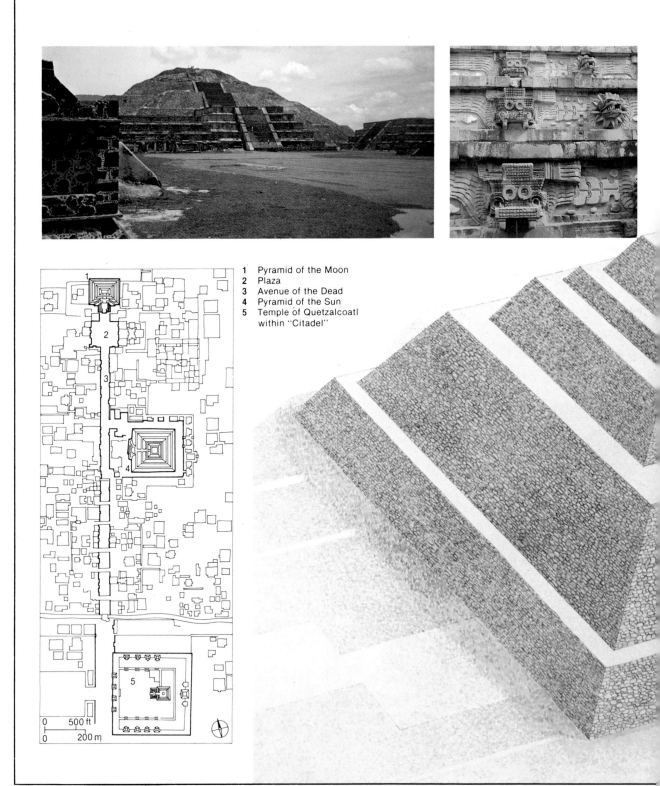

1 Pyramid of the Moon
2 Plaza
3 Avenue of the Dead
4 Pyramid of the Sun
5 Temple of Quetzalcoatl
  within "Citadel"

0   500 ft
0   200 m

The Pyramid of the Moon is not a true pyramid but is truncated to give space for a temple on top. It is one of two principal pyramids at Teotihuacán, the most regular and largest of all pre-Columbian American ritual sites. The grid pattern of avenues, temples and pyramids, workshops, and houses covered 8 square miles, a larger area than imperial Rome (see plan, left).

There was an old tradition in Mexico of building on a mound. Possibly these pyramid structures are tied to this or they were developed as part of a monumental ritual architecture.

During its early history (1st century BC) Teotihuacán was not a city. It was a center for ritual ceremonies for the surrounding farmers. They worshiped Nature and believed that the powers of Nature could be good or evil and needed to be worshiped in order to persuade them to act for the public benefit. Worship included symbolic acts such as human sacrifice, offering presents and prayers.

The Pyramids were used for religious processions and the ceremonies took place at the top. The great ceremonies took place in accordance with the solar year. The Sun Pyramid was the first to be built. It was sited on an axis with the midday sun at Midsummer. The Moon Pyramid stands at the head of the Road of the Dead. The Pyramid of the Sun, Pyramid of the Moon, the shrines lining the Avenue of the Dead and the smaller Pyramid-Temple of Quetzalcoatl, at the interesection of the Avenue and the main East-West streets were all built in the 1st and 2nd centuries AD. The Pyramid of the Moon is almost 200 feet high and stands at the head of the main processional thoroughfare. The first stage of the staircase up the ceremonial platforms demonstrates the talud–tablero device typical of Teotihuacán architecture – a rectangular panel with raised borders (tablero) alternating with a narrower sloping band (talud).

The techniques of the Stone Age were still used in the stone sculpture which decorates the facade of the Palace or the Quetzalcoatl, or Plumed Serpent (left). The serpent's head alternates with one which may be the Rain God. It is likely that the sculptures were once painted in vivid colours. Clay figures were also used as well as murals to ornament the structure.

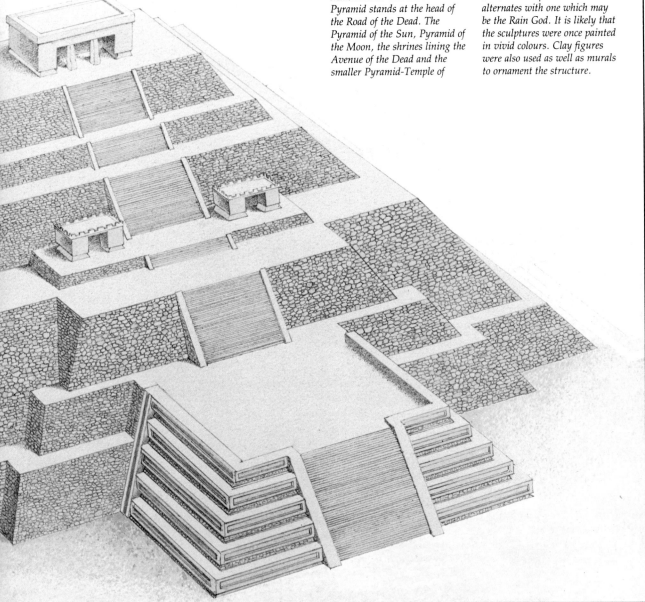

European cathedrals and the sacred mounds of Indus. The plan of Teotihuacán, for example, reflected the divisions of the universe as portrayed by Tezcatlipoca: it was divided into four parts, with four avenues meeting in a central square, the political and economic heart of the city. Dualities in nature were displayed among the Aztecs by siting the temples next to each other on a single ziggurat. For example gods of war and rain – symbols of survival – sat side by side on the Templo Mayor of México-Tenochtitlán (1521).

The pyramids and ziggurats were solid, like those of Mesopotamia. The structure was simple: it was built up with rubble, stone and earth, finished with a facing of stone or brick, which was plastered and colored. In Mexico, construction was in volcanic rock, as well as adobe brick made from sun-dried clay; and in northern Yucatán in an easily-worked limestone. Further south, in Peru mostly adobe brick was used, but also black andesite, Yucay limestone and diorite porphyry.

THE PYRAMID OF THE MOON, TEOTIHUACÁN

From above, Teotihuacán is a beautifully organized relief in rectilinear, abstract geometry. It conveys, at a glimpse, the central theme of the classical period of pre-Columbian architecture. A pyramid is an abstract form, but it was stepped, with a flat top where the house of the god could be built, accessible from the plaza below by flights of steps. The abstract object, such as the door which opens to reveal a hall, comes alive; people walk up it and enjoy the view. The platforms, acting as resting places on the way up, give modeling to the form, and the flights of steps reflect the axial plan of the city; the 2-mile (3-kilometer) avenue which takes you first to the plaza in front of the Citadel, and then to the pyramid, continues up to the front of the pyramid, culminating in a single point. Thus the flight of steps, required for access, assumes an importance extending to the plan of the entire city. It introduces a sense of occasion to the pilgrimage and completes an avenue.

Similarly other parts of Teotihuacán act together to one end, providing a form around which the rest of the city could be orderly assembled. With the exception of some palace walls round a courtyard, the houses in the city were completely destroyed. But the Pyramids of the Sun and Moon built in the 1st or 2nd century AD and the outline of the plaza and avenue resisted destruction. The steps (platforms) of the pyramid of the Moon continue as a highly-decorated and sculptured framework, several yards high, defining the plaza and establishing the edges of the long avenue. The avenue was the spine around which the structure of Teotihuacán was planned, and beside which could be sited the major buildings – the Citadel, the Sun Pyramid, the shrines and palaces, creating the enclosure of the central space. But order is achieved through the repetition of forms emanating from and defined by the platforms of the Moon Pyramid.

DEVELOPMENT OF THE STYLE

The pyramid, like the cube, is one of the great universal forms in architecture. It is seen at its finest – in Middle America for instance – where strong sunlight reveals its simplicity of shape in light and dark and casts its pointed shadow on the land. Like a sundial's, this shadow moves round with time. The cultures that have been preoccupied with the pyramid and ziggurat have also been deeply preoccupied with man's position in space and time. Their peoples attempted to orient their plans and important structures according to cosmic principles and by the position of celestial bodies. Such cultures were usually highly advanced in mathematics – the Egyptians, for instance, who were building their pyramids in 2700 BC, and the Sumerians, whose ziggurats appeared earlier (the ziggurat at Ur, however, in 2125 BC). The ziggurats of the Indus civilization, the pyramid of Silbury Hill at Avebury, England (c. 3000 BC), and the Buddhist temple-pyramids at Sanchi, India (c. 20 BC–AD 20), and Borobudur, Java (AD c. 800), all betray the same preoccupation with time and space.

The Mayans, to the east of the Teotihuacán and Aztec area in central Mexico, were both mathematically-minded and keenly interested in astronomy. They invented an accurate calendar, based on a 365-day year, and a concurrent 260-day religious cycle. The two systems coincided every 52 years, and the ending of a cycle was regarded as a most significant moment in time, to be celebrated by a renewal of spiritual activity and the rebuilding of religious monuments.

DEVELOPMENT OF THE AMERICAN PYRAMID

One early "pyramid" in Middle America is unique in being circular in form, and was built in the middle of Mexico, at Cuicuilco, in the 1st century AD, with four platforms, and a temple at the top. Another great work, the Mayan Pyramid E VII Sub at Uaxactún, has the more familiar square plan and four flights of steps to the summit. Both were influential in the development of pre-Columbian architecture. The Classic period (AD 100–900) represents the climax of pre-Columbian architecture, and includes the great Teotihuacán period of building between AD 150 and 350. Further south came the rise of new centers of building in Peru, at Paracas and Nasca in the south, and in Noshe and Moche in the north and, before the empire of the Incas, the Temple of the Sun, Moche

Oval Pyramid, Uxmal (600–900). One of the pure geometric forms, the pyramid is at its best when strong light reveals the simplicity of its shape

(800), the Gate of the Sun, Tiahuanaco (1000–1200), and the Fortress, Paramonga (1200–1400). Meanwhile the Mayans made highly sophisticated advances in ziggurat architecture, for example at the vast Temple I, Tikal (c. 500) and the Temple-Palace at Uaxactún, which began as three temples on a single, square platform, and ended as an ambitious collection of temples, shrines and palaces, accompanied by rich sculpture and brightly-colored mosaics. Little escaped the sculptor's tool: steps, platforms, vaulted roofs are all decorated. The Palace of the Governors, Uxmal (c. 900), built on a large three-stage ziggurat, is as fine an example of structural architecture and of architectural sculpture as can be found in Mayan civilization. Unusual, too, are the temples of the Mayan Río Bac region, where it is difficult to separate architecture and sculpture in the towers which are portraits of gods, and staircases which are the bodies of the gods.

Middle American architecture declined at the end of the Classic period with the supremacy of the warlike Toltecs and was only temporarily restored with the rise of the Aztecs in the 14th century, founding the capitals of Tenochtitlán; this great period of rebuilding ended forever with the arrival of Cortés.

Gate of the Sun, Tiahuanaco, Bolivia. This religious gateway predates the Inca empire by 400 years or more

Palace of the Governors, Uxmal. The mask of the rain god Chac is one of the sculpture motifs. A Mayan corbeled arch divides two blocks

CHAPTER 7

Romanesque

Quite suddenly, in the space of a hundred years or so, Romanesque architecture spread across the European continent and beyond. The Church of the Apostles, Cologne (c. 1190–c. 1220), the Cathedral of Santiago de Compostela, Spain (1075–1211), and Durham Cathedral, England (1093–1133), are some of the best examples of the style.

How quickly ideas travel. From the short, square, Classical plan, with a dome over its center – so popular in the Byzantine empire in the 11th and 12th centuries

Santiago de Compostela, Spain, portal. One of the few pure Romanesque buildings in Spain, and the finest

– the nave of the church is suddenly pulled out like a telescope and transformed with a long, narrow, tall and bare interior and sheer walls. The circular plan is relegated to the east end, behind the altar; and the Latin cross plan develops, often with a tower over the crossing-point – but with a pyramidal roof rather than a dome. Two towers often flank the west end. Windows become larger and longer, particularly in the apse; there are clerestories above the aisles; the flying buttress is concealed in the double-story aisles; and abbeys now have cloisters.

There are many influences towards the Romanesque. Charlemagne was one; he entered Italy in 773, went to Rome, and on his way back visited Ravenna, where he saw the Byzantine architecture. He was so impressed that he commissioned a replica of S. Vitale; Charlemagne was a great patron of the arts.

In the next century, the Muslims landed in Sicily, formerly part of the Byzantine empire; the Pisan capture of Palermo in 1602 may have led to Byzantine-style striped marble being used at Pisa. Pisa now rivaled Venice and Genoa (both closely associated with Byzantium) as a center of trade – a good way of exchanging ideas. There are a number of striped marble churches close to Genoa – one for instance at Porto Venere, near Spezia.

A FRENCH STYLE

But many other influences shaped the development of Romanesque. It was primarily a French style – only there did it mature into a strong style with an influence of its own, leading on to Gothic. In France it was the church which changed the direction of architecture. At that time power was concentrated in the church, the center of education and learning. In the early 10th century the Abbey of Cluny was founded in Burgundy; it was to become the most influential monastery in Europe. Its renewal and inspiration were transmitted to architecture, and so there appeared pure Romanesque buildings of exquisite beauty such as La Madeleine at Vézelay, and Autun Cathedral. La Madeleine was begun in 1096 and completed, like Autun, in 1132; they were within about 45 miles of each other.

Vézelay: interior. The economical Romanesque style next takes the striped keystone direct from Byzantine vocabulary and reminds us of the mosque at Córdoba in Spain at the same time

Above: Vézelay narthex. As at Autun Cathedral, the cool, sharp background is contrasted with the exceptional wealth of detail in the capitals, tympanum sculpture, and molding

Despite decorative Byzantine influences in the stonework and windows, the foundations of Cluniac Romanesque were, as the name plainly indicates, Roman. The Roman vault provides the structural framework of the Romanesque church; but whereas the Romans saw the vault as an engineering solution to building problems the French Romanesque architects used the vault as a sculptural form. They noticed the space which the vault enclosed and shaped, and the space which lay between the structural supports in the piers. While Roman vaulting sprang from the top of the pier, the Romanesque architects saw the vault and the pier as forms flowing together as a single element, making us more aware of the space enclosed. The attention is not now arrested by the support, but drawn to the space.

Here lay the Romanesque development of the Roman vault. The barrel vault, used at Notre Dame la Grande, Poitiers (12th century), drops out of the picture, replaced by the pointed cross-vault – one of the first appears at La Madeleine. This leads in turn to the ribbed, pointed cross-vault – for example at the Abbaye-aux-Dames, Caen (1062–1125) – a device which reduced the weight of the ceiling by introducing panels between ribs. When the pointed cross-vault was used with a high nave, and the length of two aisles equaled that of one nave vault, a greatly refined version of the Roman vault had arrived. The vault and the cross-vault were married as a single element, and the roof load taken down the pier to the ground by rib extensions in the vaults. The supports became more slender, less prominent, the great height of the nave stressing the unity discovered through the delicacy of the parts. Here was the prototype of the clustered Gothic column, found, for instance, at Lincoln Cathedral, England. Cluny's spiritual dominance is reflected in the power of the long, high nave and in the economy of the structural lines. At Vézelay and at Autun, the revival of Cluny is mirrored in the generosity of spirit, the strength and airiness, and the

Autun Cathedral

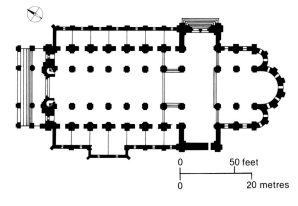

The Cathedral of Autun, in Burgundy, was built in the 12th century. Since then parts have been modified or added, as the drawing indicates. St-Lazare is not a complete and intact Romanesque church, nor is it as "typical" as some. Autun is more Classical than most Romanesque cathedrals. The fluted pilasters and the pointed arches and vaults are lighter and more delicate than the usual round arches and round columns. It is typical in its simple plan (derived from the third Abbey of Cluny) and in the frontality of approach: each part is arranged one behind the other. Each plane is parallel to the surface. This follows consistently through both the architecture and the sculpture. It is particularly clear in the sculpture, for example in the "Last Judgement" in the tympanum of the west portal (above), where the knees of God are compressed to fit the idea of designing in planes. The sculptor was Gislebertus, whose name is inscribed in the portal and whose magnificent work appears also in the capitals of figures and animals which head the main pilasters of the interior.

The original 12th-century plan is simple. The nave is long, of seven short bays; beyond the crossing with the very short transepts, two further bays lead to the semicircular apse. The nave is flanked either side by an aisle. The apse is flanked either side by apsidioles. At the west end two further bays enclosed the open porch, above which rose twin towers. The main tower above the crossing was also square.

The problems of Romanesque vault construction lay in the fact that it was a masonry method depending on the use of heavy stones, a keystone and buttressing. The medieval mason used the Roman barrel vault and the cross or groin vault, but had lost the knowledge of the Roman method using poured concrete. The results were thick walls and clearly defined spaces. The development of the rib construction, where the ribs were used as scaffolding and the infill added, together with the pointed arch opened up possibilities which were explored in the Gothic period. In this "transitional" position St-Lazare recalls the cathedral at Durham, where round Romanesque arches and massive round columns are sheltered by an early example of ribbed pointed vaulting.

0   50 feet

0   20 metres

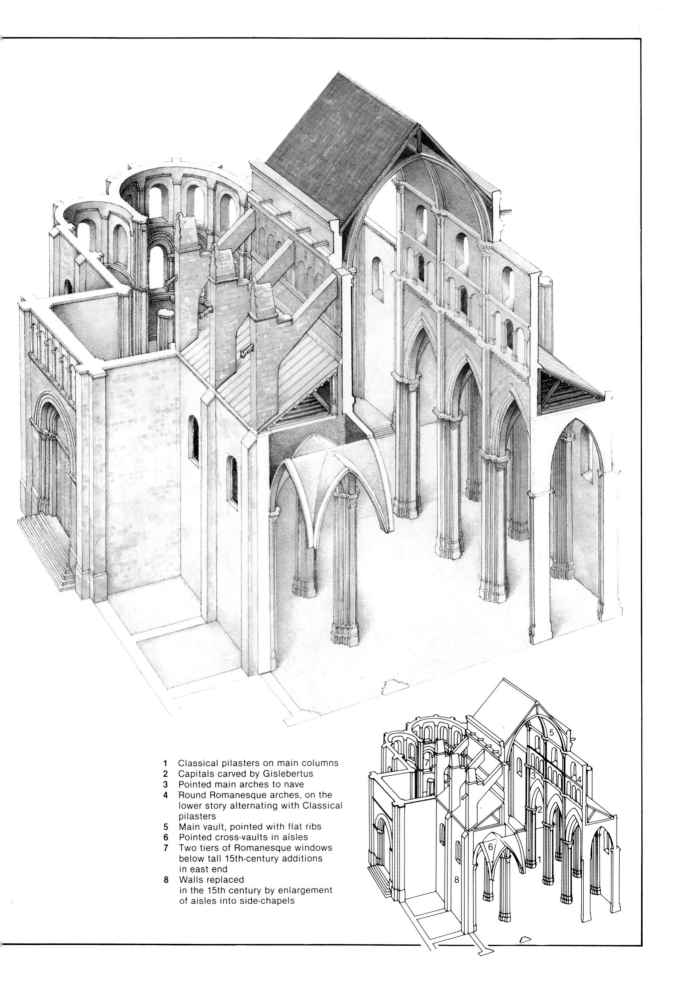

1 Classical pilasters on main columns
2 Capitals carved by Gislebertus
3 Pointed main arches to nave
4 Round Romanesque arches, on the
  lower story alternating with Classical
  pilasters
5 Main vault, pointed with flat ribs
6 Pointed cross-vaults in aisles
7 Two tiers of Romanesque windows
  below tall 15th-century additions
  in east end
8 Walls replaced
  in the 15th century by enlargement
  of aisles into side-chapels

S. Miniato al Monte, Florence, west facade. The pervasive Classical influence was central to architectural developments in Italy

vigorous sculpture surrounding the main portals. Was the same man responsible for both buildings? The name of La Madeleine's architect is not known; but the architect for Autun was Gislebertus. His genius as an architect and sculptor helped free the spirit of architecture and art.

Italian Romanesque tells a different story, interesting in quite another way. In the cathedrals at Pisa (1063–1118), Pistoia (c. 1150), and in S. Miniato al Monte, Florence (1018–62), sloping roofs betray irrepressible Classical characteristics and similarities with the roofs of early Christian buildings such as Torcello Cathedral, near Venice (c. 1008), and the basilica plan of Old St Peter in Rome (323–6). However, the interior of Pisa Cathedral also displays traces of the Roman past in its vault and its heavy, arcaded aisles; while some Romanesque buildings in north Italy, such as S. Ambrogio (c. 1080–1128), Milan, have Roman atriums.

It seems that the pervasive Classical influence was insistent enough to make all Italian architecture move slowly in the direction of the Renaissance, and not towards Romanesque or Gothic at all. Italy was flooded with influences – Norman, Byzantine, Roman – but the Roman heritage held out against change. The Classical remained central to architectural developments.

AUTUN CATHEDRAL

Autun Cathedral is the finest, the simplest, and yet intellectually the most sophisticated of all Romanesque buildings. It brought to a climax movements begun at Cluny in the 10th century, and the design of the cathedral (from c. 1120) is strongly influenced by the third Abbey church at Cluny (1088–c. 1130, demolished in 1810). Like Autun and Vézelay, the third church at Cluny had a very simple plan. The three are linked by common themes; all stress simplicity of form, and it would not be surprising to learn that Gislebertus, who was responsible for Autun, began work at Cluny, and was also involved with Vézelay.

Autun has a surprising Classical feeling, a firm discipline distinguishing it from much of the Romanesque of southwest France, which follows traditional Byzantine forms, with muddled appearance and plans. At Autun traditional forms were dropped; coherence, unity, symmetry, and a functional structure take over the architectural conception. There are many innovations but they are wholly directed to one end: order enriched by art.

A very basic ground plan, simpler than Cluny's, acts as the frame for a structure simpler than Vézelay's. Constructional details were separated in a way never before attempted. A stronger emphasis on supporting members was balanced by a great care to ensure that the more important elements did not dominate the less important; the ribs from the vaults, therefore, were neither prominent nor conspicuous. Thus the vault and its adjoining cross-vaults are supported by three very tall, flat ribs; previously they had normally been round – at Autun they became round only when turning a corner out of the nave. The pronounced Classicism at Autun also shows itself in the fluted pilasters to the reveals of the arches leading through to the aisles from the nave: the pilaster was itself an innovation, but the fluting a flashback to Greek and Roman styles. The pilasters were headed with vigorous capitals of figures and animals by Gislebertus.

The pilasters continue the generally flat treatment of the interior, in keeping with the Cluniac style, helping the structure of the building withdraw, to make a reticent background where people were as conscious of each other as they were of the sculpture. In other words, a persistent attempt was made to unify the structure and the plain surfaces of the stone walls, so that they would not intrude to disturb the calm space of the nave. A further innovation completes this unity and calm: all cross-vaults and even the main vaults were pointed, and cross-vaulting was continued throughout. The simplicity of the interior reaches a climax at the east end, behind the altar. Light pours in through large 15th-century windows which top two tiers of Romanesque arches reminiscent of the Colosseum at Rome.

Against this plain, disciplined background, Gislebertus's sculpture, magnificent, rich, stands out. Amazingly, he carried out practically all of it single-handed. Perhaps for this reason the church allowed his name to be inscribed in the place of honor on the main portal, in the middle of his own masterpiece. Lord Clark writes: "[Gislebertus] was an extrovert. He loves to tell a story, and his strength lies in his dramatic force. The row of the Damned under the feet of their Judge . . . forms a crescendo of despair. They are reduced to essentials in a way that brings them very close to the art of our time: a likeness terrifyingly confirmed by the gigantic hands that carry up the head of a sinner as if it were a piece of rubble on a building site . . . "

ELEMENTS OF THE STYLE

The essence of true Romanesque is its economy. This was the mark of Cluniac style; no unnecessary decoration; functional, plain walls vaulted and cross-vaulted, the stone cut simply, yet with great skill, to make a cool, sharp background for sculpture. At Autun, as at Vézelay, the exceptional detail over the main portal becomes dynamic in contrast with the immense calm of the space inside the building. Forms assume a greater authority when their construction remains simple. The geometry of the round columns and arches at St-Philibert, Tournus, to select an important example, is clearer for being simply constructed of small blocks of stone, and for standing within square-cornered spaces of comparable simplicity. The stone construction, and the manner in which the stones were laid, was a key to the accomplishment of satisfying sculptural forms. Where the wall of a nave was very high – St-Étienne, Nevers (c. 1083–97), is a typical example – large blocks were used for economy and speed; in columns and arches, the blocks were usually smaller; but variations in surface had an order and pattern. Similar principles apply outside; simplicity of surface and economy of materials give sculptural definition to pointed roofs and square, octagonal, or circular towers.

The plans of the three successive churches at Cluny exercised enormous influence in Europe. Strict building regulations were imposed to ensure a pervasive style, and the plan of the second church was used all over Burgundy: St-Philibert, Tournus (begun c. 950), St-Étienne, Nevers, and Ste-Trinité, Caen, are good examples. The third church at Cluny influenced the final phase of Romanesque.

However, much Romanesque was not influenced by Cluny at all. In southwest France, the starting point was the Byzantine tradition. Churches at Souillac,

Above: St-Étienne, Caen, west front. Mature Romanesque in Normandy (11th century). Built by William the Conqueror, the men's abbey is the companion of the women's abbey, Ste-Trinité

Below: Ste-Foy, Conques (1050–1130), southwest France, a pilgrimage church on the road to Santiago

Toulouse: interior of St-Saturnin (12th century). Romanesque architects saw vault and pier as forms which flowed together as a single element

Speyer Cathedral. The Byzantine origins of Aachen Cathedral influenced the development of Romanesque in Germany, the circular form in the plan being relegated to the east end

St-Pierre, Chauvigny, apse (12th century). Byzantine forms and decoration in southwest France

Conques, and Toulouse in the Dordogne and Garonne have more inward-looking plans, and circular drum forms, flat domes, and arched windows reminiscent of Byzantium. This branch of Romanesque could not develop, because of the finality of the structure.

In Spain, too, there were Byzantine influences upon such Romanesque churches as Sta María, Ripoll (1020–32) and San Tirso, Sahugún (c. 1145). Earlier churches such as San Miguel de Escalada, near León (912–13), reveal Islamic influences from Granada and Cordoba in their cloisters. Pure Romanesque shows only in a few cases, the finest being the Cathedral of Santiago de Compostela (1075–1211). Germany's most famous, and earliest, Romanesque building is Charlemagne's cathedral at Aachen, dating from 792. Its Byzantine origins influenced the development of Romanesque: Speyer Cathedral (1031–61), for example, and the Church of the Apostles, Cologne. In Britain, what Romanesque there is came from Normandy, with good examples at St Bartholomew's, London (1123–50), and Fountains Abbey, Yorkshire (c. 1135–50).

CHAPTER 8

Gothic

Strasbourg: exterior (1230–1365). With Cologne Cathedral, this is one of the finest German Gothic works

What do we picture when we speak of Gothic? Cathedrals, minsters, abbeys, churches, and chapels; spires and towers; elaborate stone constructions enclosing vast spaces, and climbing into the sky; high roofs supported on enormous columns plunging safely to the ground; architectural forms refined by the repetition of bare structural elements; highly complex windows made of thousands of pieces of stained glass, whose scenes tell a multiplicity of stories; the rich sculpture of Amiens and Rheims; and, above all, the extraordinary concentration of energy of the arch, the vault, and the buttress.

The Gothic engineering feats, exhibited at their grandest in the cathedral, were the realization of a magnificent ideal, transcending people. The cathedral was not designed to suit the place; normally the place was selected to suit the cathedral – at Lincoln the hill above the city, at Chartres the scarp overlooking the plain. Whereas many Classical buildings provided a background order to people's lives, and were calm, modest and generally low, Gothic architecture was concerned with focusing attention on a building of such magnificence that it passed beyond the human scale. The building provided humanity with a spiritual objective to aspire to.

Every cathedral, abbey, or church of the 12th to the 15th century is a unique and powerful architectural statement, a center of interest for a town or district. Yet the achievements of the Gothic style were not fully accepted until the 19th century. With the 18th-century English Gothic revival, the word Gothic ceased to be a term of abuse, meaning barbaric, and instead came to describe the style occurring between the Romanesque and Renaissance. The view of life plainly demonstrated by Gothic churches was that God was beauty; in Classical terms, a narrow attitude. If God was the center of the universe, people were marginal – and this was reflected in the jumble of timber-framed and wattle cottages huddled around the cathedrals and churches. Thus the cathedral emerges as the portrait of the age; for Gothic design could not be scaled down to benefit people in general, as the Classical style has been.

Gothic vaulting evolved from Romanesque forms. The Gothic architects developed the vaults further, working from both a square and an oblong base, giving structures greater possibilities of variation. Nevertheless, the vaulting of oblong areas proved difficult at first, and the semicircular Romanesque arch was for some time retained for diagonal or longer spans. The vaulting framework comprised intersecting stone pointed-arch ribs, supporting thin stone panels. The weight of the stone introduced downward pressure; the force of the arch voussoirs pressed outwards. Both pressures were collected by the meeting of the ribs at the angles of the vaulting compartment; the resulting oblique pressure was counteracted, and transmitted to the ground, by buttresses and flying buttresses weighted by pinnacles.

FLYING BUTTRESSES ARE DEVELOPED

The development of flying buttresses in the 12th century was the great Gothic advance. By conveying the diagonal forces from the heavy roof loads clear of the walls and down to the ground, this invention offered the architects a freedom manifesting the Gothic ideal. Not only could walls be built safely to a great height, and enormous volumes of architectural space soar to the infinite space of heaven, but also the wall, released from the role as load-bearer, could be replaced by a non-load-bearing material such as glass. Thus the flying buttresses brought lightness to the vastest structures, and cathedrals such as Beauvais (begun 1247), Amiens (1220–88), and Rheims (begun 1211), where avenues of columns and branching vaults sweep upwards, show that Gothic builders quickly exploited this new freedom.

In Gothic, structure *is* the architecture. The structure also accepts the immense richness of detail central to

St-Denis, Paris, north ambulatory (c. 1137). This is where Gothic was apparently invented, here in its early simple form

the Gothic ideal. The plans of the ecclesiastical buildings are always strong and simple, yet varied. It is the projection of the plans in three dimensions, the tremendous daring with which the construction was fearlessly carried out, the harmonious association of all visual arts, which made the architecture of this age so magnificent and memorable.

Materials were generally obtained locally. In France there was an abundance of excellent building stone, and one of the best, the fine-grained Caen stone, was widely used in northern France and in England. Flanders, Holland, and most of northern Germany used brick; the brick construction of Albi Cathedral (1282–1390) in southern France was a remarkable exception. In Spain, the stone could be carved easily, while the rich effects of cathedral architecture in central Italy stemmed from the local brown and grey stone, and white and yellow marble.

Gothic, born in France, spread rapidly to England and then back into the European continent. The

Chartres, flying buttress (13th century). The development of the flying buttress was the great innovation of the style

origins of Gothic are evident in the vaults above enormous round Romanesque columns at Durham Cathedral, England, and at Vézelay and Autun in France. The style evolved into the early, simple Gothic of St-Denis Abbey, near Paris. St-Denis is peculiarly significant, for it was here that Abbot Suger, rebuilding the church from c. 1137, apparently invented Gothic: the pointed arch, the painted glass, the bright light pouring in between the structure of columns and vaults.

Abbot Suger claimed that we only understand absolute beauty, by which he meant God, through the effect of precious and beautiful things on our senses. To him glass meant light; and in most places where the Gothic style spread, the climate induces a dull light, making big windows important. Suger found that painted glass was an ideal means of instructing the faithful, and for this reason too adopted glass on a vast scale. Suger's theory became the intellectual background of the next century, when geniuses of all kinds brought dazzling contributions to architecture, from painted glass to flying buttresses, from portal figures to gargoyles. Nevertheless, how brief was the art of the cathedral. It started and then stopped again – all in the space of three centuries. This traditional branch of Western architecture led nowhere, and ended for good.

CHARTRES CATHEDRAL

At Chartres, Suger's ideas were continued by others, and realized on a gigantic scale. It was here, after the original cathedral had burnt down, that Romanesque was transformed into the purest and most dramatic Gothic of any time. Rebuilding began in 1194. Vaulting at Chartres had to cover a space dictated by the old foundations, a space far wider than any previously encountered by Gothic architects. It was found that only the recently discovered flying buttresses could solve the structural problems posed by the vast span of the roof, and since flying buttresses now bore the load outside, there was no longer need for the inside tribune gallery above the outer aisles to provide support. So the architects abandoned it, and enlarged the clerestory so that it became a great window nearly as high as the main arcade and now, unlike Romanesque examples, brought down close to the nave. So successful was this innovation that it was promptly adopted in other cathedrals, including Rheims and Amiens.

Two views convey the vastness of Chartres. From the plain southwest of Paris, its silhouette is sighted from the far distance; the other view comes after the long climb to the top of the hill, through narrow, winding streets; with the last corner turned, there is the astonishing spectacle of the west front (c. 1150), seen across a large flat forecourt.

The forecourt is unusual in French cathedral architecture – and indeed throughout the European continent. It is reminiscent of an English cathedral setting, where a carefully arranged close is framed with terraces of houses – most perfectly at Winchester (begun 1070), Salisbury (begun c. 1220), and Canterbury (begun c. 1070). On the European continent, however, the cathedral normally mingles with its town surroundings just like the library, market hall, or important public buildings. But at Chartres, the space before the cathedral allows the spectator to observe its majesty.

The cathedral often functioned as a town meeting place. Chartres Cathedral, on a plateau with space all around it, was ideal for this purpose. Cathedrals were also centers of education; at Chartres there was a school of philosophy devoted to Aristotle and Plato. Chartres is a masterpiece of harmonious proportion, and some very complex structural design was used to create it.

Church sculpture conveyed information. The figures around the main portal at Chartres include Aristotle and Pythagoras; and there is a detailed study of musical instruments. The figures, particularly those on either side of the main doorway, are works of art as perfect as the frame of the architecture; clearly superb likenesses of unusually beautiful faces. The followers of the mason who carved at Chartres must have amounted to an army of sculptors, for the column figure spread to Rheims and Amiens; to León (1255–1303); to Strasbourg (begun 1230) and Bamberg (1185–1237); to Westminster (rebuilt 1245–69) and Lincoln (rebuilt 1192–1320).

For stained glass at its most sublime, Chartres is again unsurpassed. We are surrounded by the blues, reds and greens of 160 windows and we walk through and on their intricate colored light flooding the stone floors. The stories these pictures tell are often too complex for us to follow; yet for medieval people, many of whom could not read, the meaning was clear.

INTERNATIONAL GOTHIC

There were two fundamental differences between the styles of those great partners in Gothic, France and England. The French cathedral began as a religious meeting place within a town, where the clergy lived. The English cathedral originated as a monastery, separate from the town, with the clergy living in the cathedral environs. The church was at the heart of a complex environment, for there had also to be living quarters, dining rooms, kitchens, often a choir school and sometimes a chapter house.

Chartres Cathedral

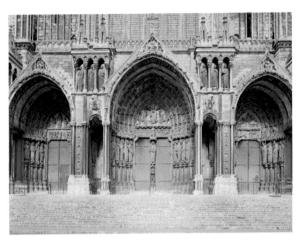

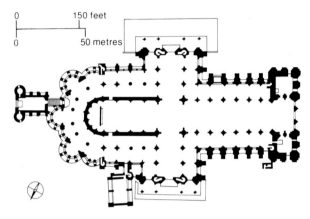

0   150 feet

0   50 metres

The advantages inherent in the use of the pointed arch and ribbed vault can be seen in the work of the Gothic cathedral masons, in particular the great cathedrals of England and of northern France – Rheims, Amiens, Beauvais, for example, and, perhaps the best known, the Cathedral of Notre Dame in Chartres.

The new flexiblity in structure enabled the designer to go round corners easily, to reduce the amount of masonry needed. With the support of flying buttresses it was possible to go further and to refine the building down to an almost skeleton structure. The walls became glass, the supporting members fine clusters of shafts and the height could be increased to give the building a greater elegance.

The English Gothic masons, while accepting the ideas from the Île de France cathedrals, were more interested in the horizontal emphasis in buildings, which meant that they did not build so tall but naves tended to be longer, and in the development of the rib vault in terms of the patterns and decorative effects of liernes, fans and bosses. Again the horizontal is stressed by the

longitudinal rib. The advances in technical skill allowed the masons to explore a variety of window tracery from early plate windows, through to the more severe, panelled effect of English Perpendicular (see p. 60). The stained glass that is the glory of Chartres and other cathedrals had a didactic as well as a decorative function (right: a window in the west end, showing the life of the young Jesus).

Sculpture became freer and more expressive. The figures are no longer fixed within the vertical plane, but project into space and are sculpted in the round. The figures on the south portal at Chartres (above), while now taking the place of columns, are also becoming more naturalistic in form. The Gothic column-figure spread from Chartres to cathedral portals elsewhere in France, in Spain, England and Germany.

1 Nave	
2 Aisle	
3 Nave arcade	**9** Molding on arch
4 Triforium	**10** Vaulting ribs
5 Clerestory	**11** Vaulting panels
6 Pier	**12** Buttress
7 Capital	**13** Flying Buttress
8 Shaft of column	**14** Wooden roof

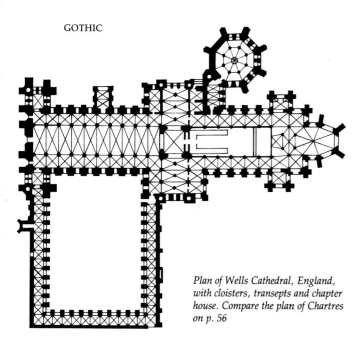

Plan of Wells Cathedral, England, with cloisters, transepts and chapter house. Compare the plan of Chartres on p. 56

Wells, west front. The English cathedral was self-contained and separate from the town, unlike its French counterpart

Winchester: the nave. An avenue of structural "trees" and overhead "branches" make the lightest possible covering for the faithful

The English cathedral plan was almost always a strongly defined cross, as at Wells (c. 1180–1485), Lincoln, Winchester, and Ely (c. 1080); at Canterbury and Salisbury there were two crosses. But in French cathedrals, the cross is rarely indicated. Rouen (1202–30) and Laon (1160–1225) have cross plans, and Chartres merely the beginning of one.

Nevertheless, the French had a powerful influence on English Gothic in the 12th and 13th centuries, and on most of the rest of Europe from the 13th to the 15th centuries. The influence of English Gothic, on the other hand, was negligible abroad, but affected educational and domestic architecture at home. The cathedral cloister and quadrangle form went into the early monastic colleges of Oxford and Cambridge, and to such collegiate schools as Eton and Winchester.

Some cathedral details led to sophisticated developments in English and Continental domestic architecture. They can be traced back to Chartres, and the consequences of the flying buttresses. The elevation of Chartres' nave explains this. At the top, there is a tall clerestory of stained glass above the narrow triforium and the arcade below. A stone mullion between the pairs of clerestory windows acted as a short column supporting the stonework above. This mullion developed in two ways. At Amiens and Rheims, the single thick mullion splits up into a number of slender mullions – the "trunk" becomes "branches" – delicate tracery, of which some of the finest is in the rose windows of many east and west fronts. But the stone column, or prop for the stone lintel over windows, is also widespread in domestic architecture, whether in the manor house or cottage, whether in wood or stone. Examples in wood range from the Hôtel-Dieu at Beaune in Burgundy (c. 1443) to the ubiquitous timber frame and wattle that spread across northern Europe; examples in stone vary from Hardwick Hall, England (1590–96), to the Doge's Palace, Venice (14th century).

In no other country was Gothic as pure as in France and England. In Spain, Portugal, Italy, Germany, Scandinavia, and the Low Countries, Gothic was clouded by other influences. In Spain the Islamic style remained strong; in Italy there was the Classical influence; in Germany Romanesque; and in the Low Countries the stone of French Gothic was replaced, on a smaller scale, by brick.

Spanish Gothic began c. 1210 and was most highly developed in Catalonia. Despite the influence of French buildings, the grand scale of the single-span vaulted interiors was, as at Gerona (begun 1312), specifically Spanish in character. At León Cathedral, the expanse of the window openings and the slenderness of the piers surpassed León's prototype, Amiens. Islamic influence was obvious in such Muslim features as the horseshoe arch, and pierced stone tracery. The most delicate example of this tracery, as varied and intricate as white lace, was in the cloisters of Batalha, Portugal (begun 1387), where it screens the authentic Gothic behind. The cloister was a traditional Islamic form (not to be confused with the English, residential, cloister) while the compactness of the plan and structure at Batalha is unmistakably French. The encounter, and natural harmony, of the Islamic and Gothic styles created a masterpiece of architecture.

Similar astonishing harmonies occur in the association of Classical, Gothic, and Islamic influences at the Doge's Palace, Venice; and of Gothic and Romanesque influences in the cathedrals at Orvieto (1290–1330) and

Batalha, Portugal, cloisters (1387–1475). Islamic influence, at its most delicate here, was very evident also in Spain and Italy

Amiens, transept and rose window. The enlarged clerestory windows were made possible by the invention of the flying buttress

Siena (c. 1226–1380). At the Doge's Palace, a firm Classical form, with a central courtyard, is constructed from superb two-tier Gothic *pilotis* (columns). The cathedral structure is copied, triforium above, arcade below; and in the plain facade over the triforium, with its memories of Islamic patterning, are spaced at intervals the large and familiar Gothic cathedral windows. Yet, for all this, in the background is that powerful Classical presence, as it is in so much Italian Gothic – a restraining influence on the development of the campanile, or on the forms of Florence Cathedral, with its horizontal emphasis upon cornices, pediments, striped marble, porticos, and the proportions of windows. The Classical frame brought Italian Gothic architecture within sight of the Renaissance. In some buildings, however, such as Milan Cathedral (1387–1483), which was partly designed by a group

Siena Cathedral (c. 1226–1380). A harmony of Gothic and Romanesque styles shows the versatility of the Gothic forms

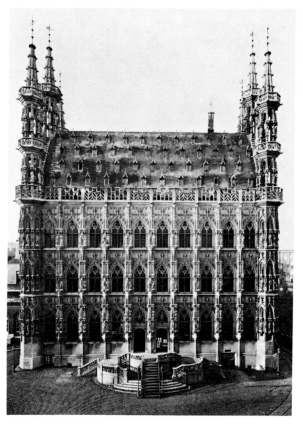

Louvain City Hall (15th century): Brabantine Gothic. An example of Gothic influence on secular building in the Low Countries

of German architects, the conflict between Classical and Gothic was never resolved.

German Gothic, which followed the French late (as Chartres was nearing completion, Romanesque chapels were still arising in Cologne), had difficulty in throwing off the heaviness of tradition, and never attained the simplicity of France and England. The great French Gothic period of the 13th century is reflected in the finest German works, Cologne (from

King's College Chapel, Cambridge (finished 1515): Perpendicular. A more direct visual connection between heaven and earth cannot be made

1248) and Strasbourg cathedrals, and in Utrecht Cathedral, built in the mid-13th century. But the heaviness which overtakes the cathedrals at Freiburg-im-Breisgau and Nuremberg, both begun in the 14th century, is reflected in Milan. This heaviness partly originated in the "Flamboyant" style of 14th-century French Gothic (the equivalent of England's "Decorated" style), as seen at Rouen in the cathedral west front. This style led to the Brabantine Gothic of Holland and Belgium, to Antwerp Cathedral and later additions to that of Utrecht, and finally to the 16th-century public buildings – town halls and business centers – of the Low Countries.

The purity and originality of the best French Gothic began to disappear at the beginning of the 14th century, although the "Flamboyant" style continued into the 16th century, when Italy was in the middle of the Renaissance. Only in 15th-century England did Gothic architecture, with the "Perpendicular" style, find a greater purity than any previous period anywhere in the chapels of King's College, Cambridge, St George, Windsor, and the superb later 15th-century Divinity School, Oxford.

CHAPTER 9

Renaissance

When you look at a building of the Renaissance period in Italy, you are looking at the design of one man. This fact, as much as any other, accounts for the unique imagination and humanity of the architecture. With the rare exception of an individual such as Gislebertus, it is difficult to perceive the work of one man in the huge Gothic cathedrals, for they were the product of a team, not of the genius of one man. The Gothic style, however, never took possession of the Italians, and the horizontal emphasis of the Classical past remained in control during the Romanesque period. The fundamental difference of attitude between the Gothic and Renaissance periods was that the dimensions of one architecture were ruled by the scale of God and engineering considerations, while the dimensions of the second were ruled by the scale of man and aesthetics. Renaissance buildings are small; their size is regulated only by practical and aesthetic necessities.

With the Renaissance it is as if Roman ideas and inventions are adopted by people as civilized as the ancient Greeks; the architecture is precise, fastidious and humane. It is the style of individuals with independent minds; it emerged from the independent courts in small independent cities and towns in medieval Italy. In such an atmosphere it was easier to encourage art, and for the independent mind of the artist to flourish and show his genius, and his imagination was more quickly recognized.

Early 15th-century Florence was the original and most important of these courts which sprang up, particularly in the north of Italy.

FLORENCE PREEMINENT
Florence, like Genoa, was a great trading center; in consequence the Florentines had enormous confidence in themselves as a race and as individuals. The Florentines believed that they had the power and the genius to rival their Roman ancestors, the memory of whom lay all around them in Roman ruins. These ruins led to a curiosity about the past, to a desire to rebuild and do better, and so to a competitive spirit. Artists enjoy competition; they encourage criticism

and are invigorated by an exchange of ideas. This spirit was the inspiration of the Renaissance.

The Florentines were also rich. The combination of riches and taste created excellent patrons of architecture and art – patrons who would take risks. It is against this discriminating background that an architecture for individuals, by individuals, was born. The Florentine patron wanted good design as he wanted great art, and he went to great lengths to get it – for example by holding competitions. This is how he found Lorenzo Ghiberti (c. 1378–1455) and Filippo Brunelleschi (1377–1446). But all these extraordinary architects, each with an independent outlook, returned to the Roman heritage for their point of departure. This strength of tradition held together such independent minds, and the architecture which they created, within the single frame of a harmonious order. Two fine qualities – independence and order – between them created the Renaissance style.

AN AGE OF DISCOVERIES
The Renaissance is also a story of discovery, a search for truth through art. Ghiberti, Brunelleschi, Alberti, Leonardo da Vinci, Donatello, Piero della Francesca, Masaccio – all were explorers. In fact the discoveries of the time – new lands, the compass, the printing press, gunpowder – all led, in one way or another, to a single end: an upheaval in which man and the church were revalued in relation to each other. Accepted dogmas were reassessed, as were accepted theories of design.

Artists scrutinized accepted methods in their search for new methods. Brunelleschi's examinations of the Roman vault led to his amazing invention for the double-shell dome (begun 1420) of Florence Cathedral. Printing spread the writings of the Classical Roman architect Vitruvius and of contemporaries such as Alberti to a wide circle of artists. Brunelleschi was fascinated by structure, and by the connections between past and present. Alberti was fascinated by beauty, and saw a link between the importance of man in the social structure and the importance of the column in the structure of architecture; for this reason he regarded the column as the primary element of architecture.

Florence Cathedral. The double-shell structure of the dome was one of the great inventions (by Brunelleschi) of this mind-searching period

Above: Bramante's Tempietto of S. Pietro in Montorio, Rome, and (below) interior detail of his Baptistery of S. Satiro, Milan. Unlike Gothic cathedrals, Renaissance works are the contributions of individual artists

Donato Bramante (1444–1514), who was a painter before he was an architect, saw architectural design in terms of planes and spaces as he might have seen a painting. While he used his gifts as a painter to create the illusion of a huge Greek cross on a restricted site in his remodeling of S. Satiro, Milan (begun 1482), his most significant work there was the Baptistery, planned as a Greek cross inside a square, inside a

Florence Cathedral: one of the "eye" windows in the cupola, showing the Nativity by Paolo Uccello (1444)

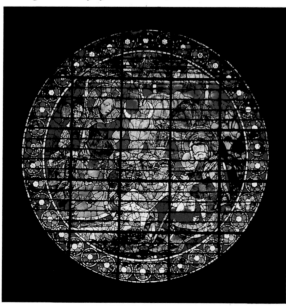

circle. This little building led on to the circular Tempietto (1502) at S. Pietro in Montorio, which in turn led to an early idea for St Peter's, Rome. His conception for the Baptistery embodied his belief that good modern architecture grew out of good ancient architecture: three perfect forms were selected for use in the plan.

Another milestone was the work of Ghiberti, particularly the work between 1401 and 1452 on his two bronze doors for the Baptistery at Florence Cathedral: the figures were cast in relief and the background space was created by perspective. This rediscovery of perspective was central to a new visual consciousness.

BRUNELLESCHI AND ALBERTI

However, probably the most important figure was Brunelleschi. He studied the details of Roman construction and was able to see afresh the principles which governed them; he extracted the essence from ponderous Roman structures, omitting unnecessary weight, and leaving only the light bones.

Sta Maria Novella, Florence (1470). The façade proportions, like those of the plan and volumes within, derive from the square

Baptistery Doors, Florence: the Gate of Paradise. Ghiberti's genius was discovered by the competitive spirit of an artistic age. The relief itself rediscovered perspective from the Greeks

This was how he came to use Roman methods with such style. At the exquisitely delicate Ospedale degli Innocenti (1419–44) and at the Pazzi Chapel (begun 1429) the results of his research can be observed: a beautiful new lightness and airiness of detail and line suddenly touch down like a bird among the heavy gloom of its contemporary surroundings. In two Florence churches – S. Lorenzo (begun 1419) and S. Spirito (begun 1436) – the Roman principles he unearthed were subjected to a mathematical analysis; using the Latin cross, and taking the square of its crossing as his basic unit, he created a pattern of squares from which he derived the plans of both churches. Brunelleschi's geometry was always of the purest: the square and the cube, rather than the rectangle, the hemisphere and the circle, rather than pointed domes and arches.

Brunelleschi was interested in sculptural form in both architecture and sculpture. Leone Battista Alberti (1404–72), whose working life overlapped with Brunelleschi's, was the first Renaissance theorist, and theorist first and architect second; he was also a painter and sculptor. Like Brunelleschi, he wanted to formulate a new architectural language in which there was a prescribed vocabulary of parts that had to be adhered to by others. He saw the connection between the parts, and the language had to be followed exactly if the aesthetic objectives were to be met correctly. He translated Vitruvius, and his great book of architecture, *De re aedificatoria* (1452), supplied a coherent theory of the five Classical Orders. He showed that beauty depends on a mathematical system of proportions; listed aesthetic rules, and defined beauty as "a harmony and concord of all the parts." His buildings demonstrate this rational approach: the proportions of his façade for Sta Maria Novella, Florence (1456–70), are entirely derived from the square.

The Pazzi Chapel, Florence

The small scale of the Pazzi Chap
can be appreciated from
the plan (below) of the Sta Croce
monastery, of which it is part;
it lies in the southern corner
of the complex.

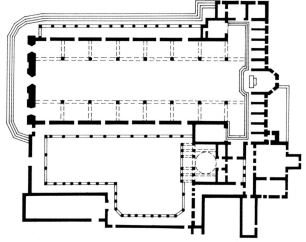

Brunelleschi's Pazzi Chapel (1429–61) contains the ideas of his maturity. It is a refinement of his earlier building, the Old Sacristy at San Lorenzo, and his handling of the modular plan is more complex while the interior detailing is simpler and more restrained. The reason for this is that he appears to have managed to keep control over the interior decoration of the chapel.

It seems certain that Brunelleschi did not believe in any decorations which would conflict with the unity of his architecture. He relied on color, the contrast of the gray pietra serena with the cream plaster, to emphasize the geometry of the forms – square, circle, cube and hemisphere. The painted terracotta reliefs of the evangelists are enclosed in roundels and set to enhance the architecture.

The Chapel was built as a private memorial chapel but also was planned to be used as part of the monastery of Sta Croce. The building was not finished at Brunelleschi's death in 1446, and there is some doubt as to whether the upper part and the dome are according to his plans. But his use of Roman Classical forms, the pilasters and the triumphal arch on three successive walls leading to the altar, illustrates the extent to which Renaissance architects borrowed these antique forms and adapted them for their own use.

Brunelleschi was fascinated by the geometry of architecture. The plan (far right) of this very influential building incorporates a progression of squares from the overall plan (which contains the loggia as well) to the central space below the dome which is treated as a square, the square altar area and the square altar. It is these shapes and, above, the circles and hemispheres created by the roof forms, that are picked out by the gray stone and reflected in the patterns inlaid in the marble floor.

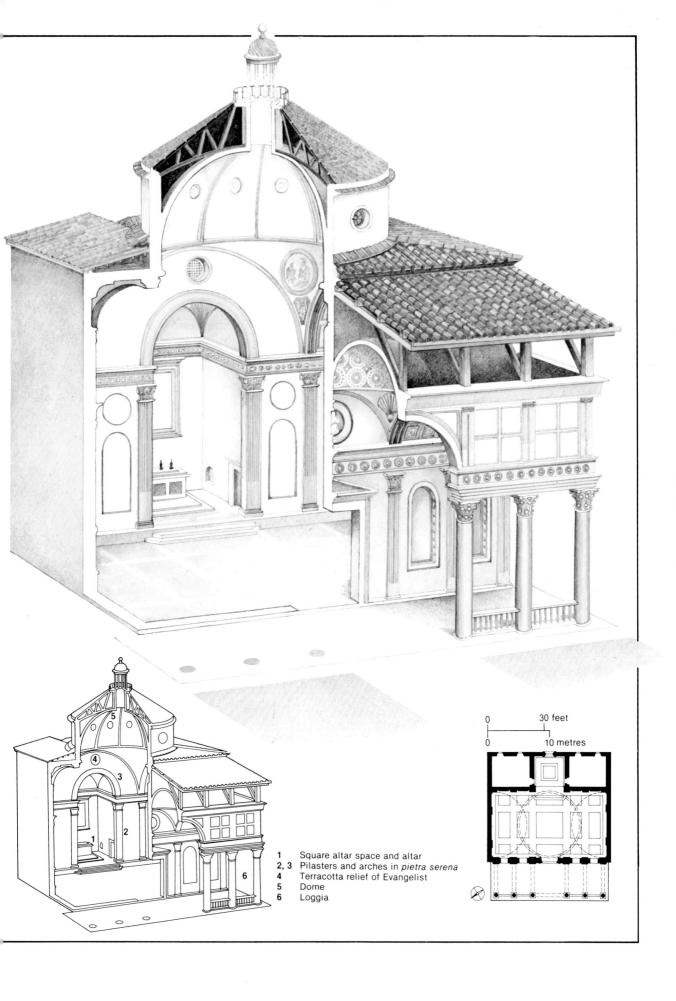

1   Square altar space and altar
2, 3 Pilasters and arches in *pietra serena*
4   Terracotta relief of Evangelist
5   Dome
6   Loggia

0   30 feet
0   10 metres

These architects were aided by superb materials, similar to those the ancient Greeks used in their precision architecture. They were well supplied with excellent marble and stone – white *Luna* marble from Carrara (Tuscany), yellow and white marble from around Siena, multicolored marbles from Genoa, travertine from near Tivoli (the finest of the many varieties of stone near Rome). Renaissance builders also found ancient ruins a source of materials which could be reused; and Venice could obtain anything by boat.

THE PAZZI CHAPEL, FLORENCE

Imagine a three-dimensional geometrical diagram drawn in dark gray ink on white paper: the arch, and the cube mounted by the hemisphere. This concept inspired Filippo Brunelleschi's superb Pazzi Chapel, begun in 1429, the dome (1459) and the loggia (1461) completed much later. A tiny structure, hidden at the end of the cloisters of Sta Croce, it is nothing less than an architectural gem. The clarity of its conception had a tremendous effect on much that followed, including, in particular, Sta Maria delle Carceri, Prato, built nearly 50 years later by Giuliano da Sangallo.

The Pazzi Chapel presents a rare phenomenon, a structure where ideal geometry generates an ideal space. The plan, including the loggia, can be contained within a square. The central area of the chapel interior is also a square, as is the plan of the altar space at the back, lying on the center line of the chapel. Thus the main lines of the building's volume rely on a sequence of reducing squares. Over the chapel's central area is the dome, but the plan is enlarged to either side so that the entire space becomes a rectangle. The roof over

The Capitol, Rome: Michelangelo's giant Order. Rules made in Greece and Rome were discovered, understood, employed, then broken

these extensions of the square is barrel-vaulted at both ends, producing the semicircular form.

Brunelleschi stressed the lines of the structural forms with strong, dark gray stone, and painted the plaster surfaces between them white, thus emphasizing their nonstructural spatial properties. Brunelleschi fell in love with geometry, and communicated his inspiration through color and detail. The nonstructural spaces are smooth and plain; the structural elements richly, if simply, worked over with pilaster flutings, capitals, beautifully modeled edges to panels, and terracotta ornament. The floor is inlaid with lines defining the geometric conception, continuing the pattern of columns and pilasters as a series of rectangles around the central square that lies beneath the circle of the dome. Brunelleschi made his three forms work hard, extracting from them every possibility, whether structural, aesthetic, or spatial. In this building nothing is extraneous. The elements are separated, clearly defined by color, shape, and detail. Together, they make a sublime work of architecture.

MANNERISM

Later there came a new phase rather misleadingly called Mannerism. Firmly established rules were relaxed. There was a restlessness in the air, artists were dissatisfied with the status quo; further developments were inevitable. Michelangelo and Giulio Romano brought a new energy to the movement. Although Michelangelo persisted in regarding himself as a sculptor, his work as an architect had as great an influence as Brunelleschi's. Maybe it was because he was a highly original sculptor that he allowed no rules to contain his imagination – an artist working directly with materials is likely to have fewer preconceived notions than an artist working with precise measurements.

Michelangelo's greatest architectural achievement was, without doubt, his rebuilding of the Capitol, Rome (from 1539), a huge sequence of spaces. The sides of the forecourt are not parallel; the distortion of perspective heightens the drama, which justified breaking an old rule. Then he invented the magnificent giant order breaking another rule from Roman days, enabling him to connect two stories with a single length of column, and to impose a vertical emphasis on a long terrace. The giant order also lent magnificence to less important city buildings – the Bibliotheca Laurenziana, for instance (begun in 1525 and completed in the 1570s), where the entrance stairway breaks all conventions to meet the sculptural requirements of its position. The Mannerist movement also attracted such artists and architects as Raphael,

Above: Villa Rotunda (Capra),Vicenza, by Palladio. Four flights of steps, four terraces, four porticoes, four entrances, four facades of a cross are crowned by a dome: the perfect classical conception

Below: Bibliotheca Laurenziana, Florence, Michelangelo's staircase. The great sculptor allowed no rules to restrict his imagination

Peruzzi, Vignola, Sangallo, and Palladio. It was in fact Andrea Palladio (1508–80) who brought an entirely new direction to Renaissance architecture. He too returned to Roman origins, but to a different aspect – the Roman country house. The smallholding was once more in demand, which encouraged Palladio to incorporate farm buildings into his country houses. Through his commissions for villas he discovered connections between nature and architecture. Just as Petrarch, the 14th-century scholar who helped found the humanist movement at the outset of the Renaissance, linked human freedom with an understanding of nature, so Palladio linked buildings with the countryside, relating interior and exterior spaces.

He accomplished this by selecting two forms from

the Classical past hitherto scarcely used in the Renaissance – the portico and the single-story colonnade. He loved both forms – at the Villa Trissino, Meledo (c. 1552), and in the project for a villa for the Mocenigo family (1570), the colonnades reach out like feelers into the countryside. And so the villa, the gardens, the farm, and the barns were arranged as a total composition. Palladio said of the Villa Pisani (1544): "If one can build on a river, it will be very convenient and beautiful, because one can carry the produce at any time at small cost into the city with boats, and it will serve for the use of the house and the animals, as well as bringing coolness in summer and making a more beautiful view, and with great profit and ornament one can irrigate the possessions and the gardens and orchards which are the soul and recreation of the villa . . ."

THE RENAISSANCE TRAVELS

Books spread the Renaissance style: the writings of Vitruvius (rediscovered in 1415), Alberti, Serlio, Vignola, Palladio, and later Inigo Jones. Serlio's books, colloquial and well-illustrated, were best sellers, translated into most European languages. But differences in climate varied the style as it moved about from place to place, giving it special local characteristics. In Florence, and elsewhere in Italy, windows were small because of the heat, and courts, colonnades, and arcades (traditional forms carried on from ancient times) provided shade in the open; roofs were low-pitched because snow was rare. The absence of a visible top to buildings led to other architectural treatments of the roof – pediments, cornices, stone balustrades. In Rome, buildings were built close together for protection against the cold winters, and the cramped streets led to first-floor (*piano nobile*) living; ground floors were devoted to entrances, staircases, arches, and shops. In Venice, the sea breezes were exploited by belvederes and balconies (useful in cramped conditions, where there was no room for gardens), and rooftop and balcony gardens were highly organized; large windows made use of breezes and light – there was little possibility of sidelight in such cramped conditions. Cold winters led to chimneys, a distinctive characteristic of Venetian architecture.

In France, Renaissance and Gothic combined and, with high-pitched roofs for the greater rainfall, led to a picturesque version of the style in château architecture. In the Netherlands we find still larger windows for light (gable ends also supplied additional light in the roofs); the Dutch style is distinctive for grand detail in small buildings. The Dutch influence affected England and Scandinavia. In England, the early Renaissance was established in Elizabethan times, where Gothic and Classical combined as in France. In the Jacobean period, Classicism gradually replaced Elizabethan irregularity. In the 17th century the Palladian movement, headed by Inigo Jones (1573–1652), finally took possession. In Spain, Renaissance detail was again added to Gothic forms that were, in turn, varied by Islamic influences.

Above left: Brunelleschi's Ospedale degli Innocenti, Florence. Principles of Roman construction were seen afresh: a new lightness emerged

Below left: Azay-le-Rideau (1518–29). This Loire château shows the picturesque combination of Renaissance and Gothic styles found in France

CHAPTER 10

Baroque and Rococo

The forms and movements of Rubens' paintings, Rembrandt's lighting effects and arrangements of masses, the order and weightlessness of Bach's music all convey the spirit of Baroque. The style emerged from the Renaissance in Italy with St Peter's, Rome, in the 16th century; it was in full flood a century later with Bernini's colonnades at St Peter's (1656–67), Cortona's Sta Maria della Pace, Rome (rebuilt 1656–7), and Borromini's S. Carlo alle Quattro Fontane, Rome (1638–44, facade 1665–7). It swamped central Europe in the 18th century with such buildings as Neumünster-Stiftskirche, Würzburg (1710-19), St Nikolas, Prague (1703–52), and the Karlskirche, Vienna (1716–37).

Baroque was an emotional, sensuous architecture, a reaction against the strict aesthetic rules imposed by the Renaissance. Yet it was also released by scientific advances: the invention of projective geometry and calculus in the 17th century opened the way to untried constructions. Hence the emphasis on *geometry* in Baroque: architects could now solve highly complicated structural problems, and project complex spatial conceptions as drawings, accurately describing them for construction. Renaissance was a springboard for Baroque which displayed an uninhibited mastery of Classical principles.

THE GEOMETRY OF THE BAROQUE

Baroque makes us think of geometry, of vast volumes of space framed by geometric forms, by circles, semicircles, ovals, domes; of shapes that seem unable to stay still, bubbling outlines, concentrated creative energy fountaining out as sculpture, restless barley-sugar columns, broken pediments. We think of Michelangelo (1475–1564), Cortona (1596–1669), Bernini (1598–1680), and Borromini (1599–1667); of the Theatine Church, Munich (1663–88, facade 1765–8); of the Kinsky and other Baroque palaces, in Prague. The architecture of Baroque is immensely three-dimensional; like Gothic, it focused on the church, and spread across Europe, which Renaissance did not. Like Gothic, too, it was dramatic, but, unlike Gothic, ordered by Classical principles and by masses.

St Nikolas in Malá Strana, Prague (1703–52), by C. and K. Dientzenhofer: east end of nave, pulpit and, beyond, side chapel

Evidence of the Baroque appears very early; Leonardo da Vinci's drawings of whirlpools are portents of Baroque freedom, and his church designs in some drawings of 1489 are strongly Baroque in both conception and expression: the centralized plans, the Greek cross metamorphosed as a circle, and the perspective sketches projecting the plans as round as sculptural forms. Leonardo's vision appears to jump 50 years. Another Leonardo design, for a church in 1511, is again far ahead of its time – the beautiful plan, huge in

S. Carlo alle Quattro Fontane, Rome, facade (1665–7), by Borromini, displaying the new freedom of expression

S. Ivo, Rome, by Borromini. A theatrical stage-set effect is achieved by Baroque form externally as well as internally

scale, with sculptural masses foreshadows Michelangelo's reconstruction of St Peter's in 1546.

Michelangelo's scheme for St Peter's contained all the chief ingredients of Baroque. The Greek cross was reduced to an outline defined by circular, square, semicircular and semisquare spaces; the square form was put around them to raise interior scale to the scale of the outside world. The structure then springs from the centralized plan as piers supporting the dome. Structure in architecture embodies man's visions of form and space. The essential elements that create Baroque's magnificent spaces are combinations of the circular plan and Greek cross, the drum, pendentive and tie-bar, and the ribbed dome; in other words a harmonious fusion of the Roman Pantheon, the Byzantine, and the Renaissance of Brunelleschi. These elements were employed in Rome, for instance, at Cortona's SS. Martina e Luca (1635–50), Borromini's S. Carlo alle Quattro Fontane (begun 1633), and at Bernini's church at Castel Gandolfo (1658–61).

In 1650, however, Borromini accomplished an important break with tradition at S. Ivo, Rome, when he dispensed with the Byzantine elements of the pendentive and drum to eliminate horizontal lines, and to emphasize the vertical unity of space from the floor to the top of the dome. This innovation freed Baroque still further, and led to the sweeping forms practiced by Borromini's disciple, Guarino Guarini (1624–83), an architect, mathematician, and monk, whose exciting work influenced European architecture for the next two centuries.

BAROQUE BECOMES INTERNATIONAL
Two factors in particular turned Baroque from a movement into an international style. The first was the birth in a single decade (the 1590s) of three brilliant architects – Pietro da Cortona, Gianlorenzo Bernini, and Francesco Borromini. With scientific developments and enlightened patronage, nothing could stop them. The patrons were now not the rich merchants who brought the Renaissance into being; the patron was now the Catholic Church struggling for ascendancy with Protestantism. Great art moves emotions, as an inspired church recognized; moreover no fine abstract idea, such as Christianity, can attract a following of millions unless it is a fine and visible fact.

Most architects and artists of the time were devout Catholics, and the combination of enlightened patronage and faith in the spirit (whether of God or man) was crucial to the creation of great art. Faith supplied the drive, and both faith and a sense of theater supplied Baroque's popular appeal. No wonder Bernini is particularly identified with Baroque;

besides being an architect, sculptor, painter, composer, and writer, he was also the finest theater designer of his day. His gifts encompassed every aspect of Baroque; he was able to carry through single-handed, and control down to the smallest detail, the most ambitious projects. But he never forgot Classical teaching; this gave his buildings order, a strength dissipated in the European Baroque of the 18th century.

ST PETER'S, ROME

It is not hard to realise that St Peter's is unique: the vast volume of space trapped between dome and floor, framed by four enormous piers; the nave with its giant Corinthian pilasters; the colonnades reaching out into Rome. No plan in the world resembles the sensuous form and concentrated energy of St Peter's: richly Baroque, a Classical unity on a colossal scale, the plan focuses on a single target: the greatest church for Christ's vicar on earth.

A number of architects worked on St Peter's at different times, and mistakes were made, yet clarity of vision triumphed, transcending all else. The architectural statement evident in the plan is simple but emphatic, although St Peter's took more than 150 years to design and build. The foundation stone for Bramante's Greek cross plan was laid in 1505, but we have largely Michelangelo and Bernini to thank for its completion. You enter St Peter's Square between Bernini's colonnades; with their continuation as straight, closed colonnaded entrances to the Vatican and sacristy garden they form, perhaps appropriately, a keyhole shape. City scale and the scale of the building meet in the square. The colonnades prepare for the closed colonnades. For example, the shadows of the columns are continued by the stripes of the steps in shadow, short ramps, the light from the long windows, and shadows from the walls between. At the far end, a flight of steps lifts up like a sudden, final chord in a piece of music.

From the oval piazza, the space in front of St Peter's narrows, focusing attention on the entrance. Bernini's piazza was completed in 1667, the facade designed by Carlo Maderna in 1612. Maderna lengthened the nave at the same time, transforming Michelangelo's Greek cross into the Latin cross. This weakened the conception; the view of the dome is hidden by Maderna's facade, and Michelangelo's magnificent portico of free-standing giant columns has been lost. At the sides and back, the roundness of apse, drum, and dome remain connected parts of a single form; the last section of this form is missing. The dome itself, begun after Michelangelo's death in 1564, was also changed: it was

made more pointed by Giacomo della Porta, and finished in 1590. Sir Christopher Wren's St Paul's Cathedral (1675–1710), London, one of England's few truly Baroque buildings, was also conceived as a Greek cross, and changed to a Latin one due to official determination to incorporate a processional approach to the altar. This reduced the drama as it has at St Peter's, particularly outside, despite the huge figures 20 ft (6.1 m) high which appear scarcely more than life-size from down below. But in Rome the loss of drama is only momentary, thanks primarily to Bernini; the space he created outside is a continuation of the volume of the nave inside. And looking through the enormous theatrical *baldacchino*, or canopy (1624), by Bernini which frames the altar, one is suddenly aware of Michelangelo's four stupendous central piers, supporting the dome whose apex is 335 ft (102 m) above the floor.

St Peter's describes Baroque better than words could ever do: generosity of spirit, but not extravagance – taste, not waste. In all, eleven architects had a hand in its design, yet we find a unity of idea and purpose, a giant structure which never exceeds logic, yet raises a dome so high that it appears weightless. In the wings are Classical principles, of which Bernini's Tuscan columns are a quiet reminder.

THE DEVELOPMENT OF THE STYLE

Baroque characteristics varied according to the countries that developed and absorbed it to their traditional style. For example, Italy was entrenched in Classical traditions, and the guidelines of Brunelleschi and Alberti held good for the best part of the 17th century, as we see from the colonnades at St Peter's and from the street facade of Sta Andrea al Quirinale in Rome (1678). Bernini was a firm believer in Classical guidelines, particularly on the exterior, where his design looked up to the scale of the city; he reserved the drama, excitement and ornament for the inside, although even there his columns, pilasters, and entablatures formed a strict aesthetic frame within which to work. His influence was dominant in Italy; Italian Baroque is characterized by restraint.

France, directly influenced by the Italian Renaissance, also took the Baroque style from Italy. Italian artists such as Leonardo da Vinci, Vignola, and Serlio went to France to escape war in the early 16th century and helped to make Paris a dazzling art center. Bernini's influence dominated the later Baroque phase, supplanting earlier superficial influences from northern Italy. Bernini's design for the Louvre was selected in 1665, but his magnificent conception was not built; nevertheless, it brought Classical Baroque to the

St Peter's, Rome

Baroque architecture emerged from Italy with the building of St Peter's. The three plans illustrated of Bramante (left), Michelangelo (right) and Maderna (above) show the evolution of the ideas behind the planning of the largest and most important church in Christendom. It was thought that the old St Peter's was built on the site of the grave of St Peter, and therefore a centralized Greek cross plan could suitably express its function as a martyrium. However, this was not a suitable form for the liturgical functions of the church, so eventually Michelangelo's central plan was transformed into a Latin cross, with the building of the nave and facade by Maderna (1607–74).

The alterations Michelangelo made to the original Bramante plan, were partly structural – Bramante's piers were not large enough. However, it is also clear that Michelangelo's approach to architecture was different. Where Bramante's plan is static, Michelangelo's is full of movement. He handled architectural form as if it were sculpture. As a sculptor he was interested in making his buildings expressive, and as a result, while using the Classical language of architecture, he often used it in an unclassical way.

The architecture of St Peter's begins in the Renaissance and concludes in the era of Baroque. The wholly Baroque elements are those parts added by Bernini: the colonnade around the oval Piazza (1656–67), described by Bernini as the welcoming arms of the Church (far right), the sculptured architecture of the great brass baldacchino (below) over the altar (begun 1625), and the blaze of gold and light in the catedra he sculpted for the east wall. All three are very different. One is to do with setting, one is in itself a small piece of architecture, and one is a wall sculpture, where he manages to dissolve the wall into the sculpture.

Michelangelo's
central Greek
cross building
3 Nave and
facade by
Maderna
Dome by
Giacomo della
Porta, 1588-90
Baldachino
by Bernini

0   150   250 feet

0   50   75 metres

Versailles (1661–5), by Le Vau. The combination of Classical and Baroque came to be characteristic of French city architecture

Above: Place des Voges, Paris (1605–12), the first comprehensively planned residential square

Below: Château, Vaux-le-Vicomte, by Le Vau (1661), with gardens by Le Nôtre

attention of the French, and the east facade of the Louvre (1667–72) by Perrault is much more restrained and Classical (though a little dull) than the earlier flamboyant courtyard facade (1624–54) by Lemercier.

The combination of Classical and ornate Baroque led eventually to a characteristic French style, seen in the later Palace of Versailles (1661–5) by Le Vau, the Petit Trianon at Versailles (1762–4) by A-J Gabriel, and in the formal layout of gardens (a new departure for Baroque) such as those at Versailles (1662–90) and the Tuileries, Paris, by Le Nôtre (1664–72). An interesting example of civic design is the Place des Vosges, Paris (1605–12), the first comprehensively planned residential square, where a sequence of small châteaux is joined to form a terrace. The château of Vaux-le-Vicomte by Le Vau (1657–61) is a masterpiece, with its gardens by Le Nôtre. Le Vau also designed the Hôtel Lambert, Paris (begun 1639–44), in classically restrained late Baroque. By contrast the Hôtel Sully, Paris (1624–9), by Jean Androuet du Cerceau, is truly ornate Baroque. Among Paris churches, two fine examples, both planned round a Greek cross, are St-Louis des Invalides (1675–1706) by J. Hardouin Mansart and the Panthéon by Soufflot.

France greatly affected the Netherlands, as seen in the Nieuwe Kirk, Haarlem (1645–9), by van Campen. But by far the finest Baroque developed in Germany and Austria in the late 17th century and then spread east into Bohemia, evolving into a national style of architecture between 1670 and 1770. The significant innovation was vivid color against a white background. Baroque came from over the Alps, Rococo from France, the two styles combining to create a picture of structure and decoration, volumes of space and a myriad of detail.

Baroque provides the framework on which Rococo hangs; Rococo supplies freedom, color and movement to the more static Baroque forms; without color the unique message of Central European Baroque could not have been communicated. The symbol of earth is rocks (see for example St John Nepomuk in Munich); the symbol of heaven is the ceiling (see the ceiling paintings at the Würzburg Residenz – as startling as sudden sunlight on landscape).

ROCOCO

In Austria, the most influential architects were Johann von Hildebrandt (1668–1745) and Johann Fischer von Erlach (1656–1723), both of whom studied in Rome. The Piaristenkirche, Vienna (1716–21), by Hildebrandt shows the influence of the Italian architect Guarini, while the Karlskirche, Vienna (1716–37), was perhaps Erlach's finest work. Hildebrandt's Belvedere Palace,

Residenz, Würzburg, main staircase. The trompe-l'oeil of sculptured limbs reaching out from Tiepolo's painting is a Rococo expression of the connection between architecture, sculpture, and painting

Karlskirche, Vienna (1716–37), by Johann Fischer von Erlach. Decoration takes over from structure in the Rococo period

16,17 Above: the Abbey Church, Banz (1710–18) and (below) High Altar of the Pilgrimage Church, Vierzehnheiligen (1743–72). Rococo structure dissolves in decorative detail, cloudy grains of marble, color and gilt

Vienna (1692–4), suggests French influence, notably that of Lemercier's courtyard at the Louvre, finished half a century earlier; both the Austrians and Germans were quick to assimilate ideas from other countries.

A remarkable example of German Baroque is the Abbey Church, Banz, in northern Bavaria by Johann Dientzenhofer (1718). This building and St Margaretha, Brevnow, near Prague by Dientzenhofer's brother, Kilian (1708-15), with their pronounced Rococo characteristics – no solid walling, larger windows, structural elements reverting to the pier, as in Gothic, and vast painted ceilings of clouds, cupids, and sunny skies – led to the Rococo of Johann Neumann (1687–1753), particularly remembered for his work at Würzburg (additions to the Residenz, 1719–44) and the Pilgrimage Church of Vierzehnheiligen (1743–72), the most famous of all German Rococo churches. In this building the masculinity of Bernini's Baroque seems transformed into cumulus, blown by arbitrary whims.

CHAPTER 11

Indian Asia

For Westerners at least, Indian architecture is most mysterious: a huge temple, a single column, a tree or a mound of earth. Many extraordinary building forms were thrown up by Hindu, Buddhist, and Jain cultures: the chaitya or assembly hall, Bhaja (2nd century BC), the stupa of Borobudur, Java (8th century AD), Kailasanath Temple at Ellura (AD 750–950), and the enormous temple at Lingaraja (AD c. 1000). These towering edifices, so heavily laden with carving and sculptural reliefs that their gigantic shapes resemble the dense twigwork of a bird's nest, do have a family likeness to the late medieval cathedrals of France. As in Europe, ceremonial architecture in India eclipsed all else: secular building was relatively insignificant and few examples survive.

But when we look more closely at Indian temple architecture we discover that in almost all cases the sculpture and carving stress horizontals, suggesting steps, and the form of the structures is generally pyramidal – the Rajrajeshvara Temple, Tanjore (AD c. 1000), the Kesava Temple, Somnathpur (1268), the

Kesava Temple, Somnathpur (1268). The forms are generally pyramidal, if rounded, as the mound of the early Indus civilization

Great Temple complex of Madura (17th century), to take some examples. In other words, the inspiration for the temple or stupa is the staircase leading up to heaven. Hence the probable origins of this architecture: the Indus civilization of 2500–1500 BC, the earlier Sumerian civilization, and the ziggurat.

The Indus town was planned grid fashion; the squares of the chessboard densely packed with houses and shops, the streets orientated along the cardinal points of the compass. One square was reserved for a mound, on top of which was a citadel (the stepped Sumerian ziggurat was crowned with a temple), from which people could look beyond the walls of the town, enjoying the space of the countryside, or could look down at their home. From below in the town, the citadel provided the fixed image of a sentry guarding the spiritual beliefs of the people, and a cultural center for the town. The Indian temple met similar objectives; it manifested the patterns of everyday life and served a collective need; like the ziggurat it was stepped.

THE MAKING OF THE INDIAN STYLE

Many other influences later followed trade and military invasions, notably, Persian (via Alexander the Great), Greco-Roman, and Muslim. But strongest were the Mauryan Buddhist empire in the north (c. 300 BC) and the Bactrian Buddhist kingdoms of Gandhara and Sialkot in the northwest (c. 200 BC). Their temples, monasteries, chaityas, and stupas were designed for large groups of worshippers, for example the Great Stupa, Sanchi (2nd century BC–1st century AD), and the chaitya halls at Bhaja and Karli (1st century BC–2nd century AD). The later influence of Greco-Roman architecture shows in simpler forms – for example the chaitya at Ellura (c. 7th century) – and a more strongly emphasized structure. In Hindu and Jain architecture decoration was far more elaborate, so dense that the form of the structure disappeared beneath it, as at the Jain Dilwara Temple, Mount Abu (11th century) and the Hindu Kandariya Mahadeo Temple, Khajuraho (c. 1000). After the Buddhist culture established itself in the north it spread along the River Ganges, and then down the Indus into central India.

The earliest temples and stupas were constructed from timber, and carpentry details of structure were later translated into stone. In north India building stone – such as white marble (Rajasthan) and red sandstone (Agra) – was used as a facing to rubble infilling behind.

THE STUPA AT BOROBUDUR

When the Buddhist influence spread to southeast Asia, it also spread to Indonesia; it is at the center of this country at Borobudur in Java that the finest shrine of all (built in the 8th century) is found. This stupa, built during the late Buddhist period, is the architectural culmination of all that preceded it. From the distance, it appears a natural landmark, a hump in the countryside, a foothill to the smoking volcanoes in the background. It is, in fact, a ziggurat of vast size, growing from a severely Classical plan: the Buddhist mandala, where the circle, the central stupa (the peak), lies within the square, the ziggurat stepping up to the

Kandariya Mahadeo Temple, Khajuraho (c. 1000). Later decoration was so dense that structural form disappeared beneath it

Dilwara Temple, Mount Abu (11th century). Carpentry details from the original timber structures were translated into stone

platform at the top. Built of stone, its sides are 500 ft (152 m) at the base; it rises through five stepped faces and five enclosed galleries, built on a square plan. At the platform, three circular stepped terraces lead up to the central stupa – the world mountain that this spectacular building symbolizes flattens out at the top. On the three circular terraces, 72 small stupas, each in the shape of a bell or an upturned lotus flower, encircle the central stupa like necklaces.

Thus, including the stone base, there are in all nine stories, reflecting Indian cosmology and the Mahayana Buddhist cosmic system. The square terraces represent the world of man, the circular terraces the world of God; in the journey to the top, hundreds of sculpture panels describe the life of a royal Bodhisattva. But when the enclosed galleries end, this dazzling display ends too; the fertile valley has been left behind, the cosmic mountain has been scaled. The small stupas are all hollow and in each one can be glimpsed through perforations in the stone a Buddha looking away towards the horizon. The mound of the Indus and the ziggurat of Sumer have traveled halfway around the world; but, as ever, the structure is established by the four cardinal points of the compass, placing it within the cosmic system of the universe.

DEVELOPMENT OF THE STYLE

The strong Classical forms of the early and middle Buddhist period are clearly demonstrated at Sanchi in

The Stupa of Borobudur, Java

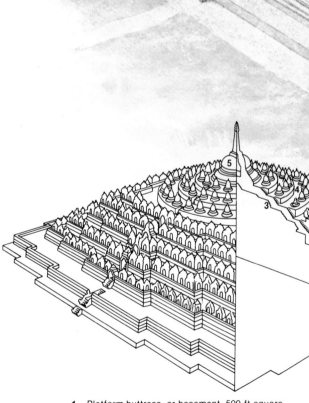

The origins of the stupa go back to the old practice of burying holy men and princes under artificial hills of earth and brick. The ashes of the Buddha himself were distributed and enshrined under eight stupas.

The Stupa of Borobudur in central Java, Indonesia, is perhaps the finest of the great Buddhist monuments of greater India. It was built in the 9th century, quite late in the period of Buddhist art, and from soon after, until the 19th century, was lost and forgotten. Its architectural form can be explained by its symbolic meaning. The nine terraces leading to the terminal stupa on the summit represent the Buddhist idea of the stages man must pass through till he can be absorbed into the Void. The plan (right) of the circle within the square, is the Buddhist mandala, the square basement platform and the five galleries representing the world of man, and the three circular platforms the world of God.

The cosmology and the purpose is reinforced by the sculptural reliefs which decorate the walls of the five galleries. The reliefs (far right) recount the story of Buddha and the acts of faith of various disciples. Even the style of the sculptures reflects the movement upwards from the busy, disorganized world of desire in the bottom, to the still, clear world of the three round terraces, the seventh, eighth and ninth planes of life, where 72 buddhas look out through the stone lattice work of 72 bell-shaped stupas, towards the horizon, and the Great Buddha is sealed under the crowning stupa.

The pilgrims climb up, past the sculptures, to the summit. Their physical pilgrimage symbolizes the spiritual pilgrimage that Buddhists have to make.

1 Platform-buttress, or basement, 500 ft square
2 Five galleries of square plan, with stone reliefs
3 Three terraces of circular plan
4 Three rings of small stupas housing Buddha figures
5 Central stupa on summit
6 Staircase to the summit

6

0   90 feet
0   30 metres

Above: Great Stupa, Sanchi (2nd century BC-1st AD). This strong form was designed to assert its presence among crowds of worshipers

Below: Lingaraja Temple, Bhuvaneshvar (7th-12th centuries AD). Decorative carving as if inspired by steps of the early ziggurats

the Great Stupa, and in Stupa II (late 2nd century BC), Stupa III (2nd–1st century BC), and Stupa I (1st century AD). The stupas, circular in plan, had a semi-elliptical stone dome to match; the structure led as naturally from the plan as in the Pantheon, Rome (contemporary with Stupa I). The plan led directly from the circular symbol of God and heaven; the unique form is both complete and continuous, like the Buddhist conception of life.

In every instance, the stupa is pure in definition and unadorned with detail. It is a mound, echoing the earlier Indus civilization; it is a round ziggurat, echoing Sumerian civilization. The staircase to the upper level and external gallery, from which at Borobudur the Buddha, posed in meditation, is half-seen through stone grilles, follows the circular plan, forming a step in the structure's section. Simpler than the ziggurat, more developed than the Indus mound, the combination of two great conceptions from the past as a shrine with a hollow interior made a perfect work of architecture. The dome, springing from the solid walls of the circular base, derives from the construction of the arch, at once indicating Greco-Roman influence.

THE INFLUENCE OF BUDDHISM

The stupa did its job beautifully and economically. But then, it was inspired by the Buddhist teachings of simplicity, modesty, and restraint in all things; it presented the essence, and manifested the Buddhist mandala in three dimensions. The Buddhist conception was total and final, as we see from the stupa in the hall at Karli (AD 120); all that could be added was space and decoration. The extraordinary Hindu temple of Lingaraja, Bhuvaneshvar, a sequence of ziggurat domes building up to a cylindrical form of immense size, could house the Mukteshvara Temple (10th century) with the same ease that the Buddhist hall at Karli houses its stupa. The simplicity of the stupa at Sanchi has vanished under layers of detail – rings of stone and a jungle of sculpture. Of course Lingaraja, like the Virupaksa Temple, Pattadakal (740) and the Great Temple of Madura, is a magnificent venture; but the shape and meaning of the great period are lost.

Buddhist architecture spread to Sri Lanka in the third century BC, and the most important stupas are the Ruvanveli Dagaba, Anuradhapura (2nd century BC) and the Thuparama Dagaba (3rd century BC), also in the ancient capital; again they display the architecture at its simplest and noblest. Buddhism spread to Burma at the same time (3rd century BC). Buddhist, Hindu and Jain influences subsequently spread across southeast Asia bringing the familiar architectural characteristics of India. Almost all buildings of real

Above: the Shwe Dagon Pagoda, Rangoon (16th-17th centuries). Architectural gems were almost always religious buildings

Below: Bodnath Stupa, Katmandu. The reassuring dome crops up again and again in an uncertain world, like the sun rising day after day

distinction are religious – the Shwe Dagon Pagoda at Rangoon in Burma (16th–17th centuries) is a particularly beautiful example of the Buddhist style. Indian influences, chiefly Buddhist and Hindu, moulded the Khmer civilization that produced the great temple shrines at Angkor, Kampuchea, notably in the 12th century. In Afghanistan, with its strong associations with Hellenistic Greece through Alexander the Great (showing, as in parts of northern India, in columns and Ionic capitals), the Buddhist influence began to penetrate in the 1st century BC. In the 5th century AD, Buddhist and Hindu stupas and temples reached Nepal – the Bodnath Stupa, Katmandu (date unknown) is a marvellous example of Buddhist design, and of extreme simplicity. Tibet came under the Buddhist influence slightly later, in the 7th century, but the pyramidal form and upturned "lotus" domes remain in the stupas and monasteries, as seen at the much later Potala "Palace", Lhasa (1642–50).

Left: Sleeping Buddha, Anuradhapura. The simplicity of form which is the Buddhist ideal is scaleless in human terms: man as part of landscape

CHAPTER 12

China and Japan

The appearance of Chinese architecture is well-known; it comes to us in tapestries, in paintings, on ceramics, in myths, legends, and old Chinese sayings. "If the wrong man uses the right means, the right means work in the wrong way." But if the right man uses the right means, the right means will work in the right way. Chinese architecture moves with the current; it is inspired by the spirit and underlying order of nature. The curving eaves of houses, pagodas, and temples, the bright blues, the reds as hot as the sun at its zenith, the bracketed framework propping up huge, sweeping roofs, the symmetery of the rectangular south-facing plans – all these have a reason.

Everything in Chinese architecture is based on the influences man faces on earth. They may be to do with the cold winter winds from Mongolia, or with the huge spaces of China, with seasons and treacherous rainfalls, with supernatural forces that must be tapped for good fortune, or with the joys of the senses and the intellect.

Chinese fascination with the rectangle and its orientation can be seen in the late Shang dynasty tombs (12th and 11th centuries BC) and in the design of hundreds of Han dynasty tiles (c. 200 BC), in which the world of man is clearly marked off from the unknown on all four sides by animal symbols – dragon (east), red phoenix (south), tiger (west), snake (north) – representing both the position of the sun and the seasons in color. These are the four elements; the fifth is the earth on which man stands. Since he found himself in a huge space, and was unable to gauge where he was, he tried to determine his position in space with greatest possible precision. This point was located in the middle of his conception of the universe, in the center of the square of the tile, a conception reproduced in building.

Thus Chinese architecture focused on man, on the square of man and the circle of nature. While the circle represented heaven, the square expressed man's territory, his intellect, his order, his house or city. The square or rectangular house-form evolved directly from its relationship with the cardinal points of the compass, not from the rectangular mud-brick house of

Above: Temple of Heaven, Peking (AD 1420). An entrance, part of the complex laid out on a longitudinal plan

Below: tea house, "Yu Yuan" Garden, Shanghai. Upturned eaves draw imaginary circles in the heavens

Tiles, eaves and bracket construction at (below) the Summer Palace, Peking; below right: Xuan Wu Lake, Nanking; bottom right: Hanchow. Dragons and other demons guard home and temple

Above: Temple of Heaven, Peking. The three circular tiers in the roofs and platforms are based on the heavenly theme represented by the circle. The eight staircases reflect points of the compass

the Near East. Then the addition of the heavens as a sixth side made a cube, a "six-sided world," as a Han dynasty book describes the universe; this cube found its expression on earth as a house. So, architecture, in focusing on man, also focused on his conception of the universe, with the square or rectangular plan orientated towards the south and applied, regardless of topography, to everything – houses, temples, pagodas, palaces, city plans, even tombs (although these faced north). From start to finish, an intellectual order was imposed upon the land.

All roofs were tiled (usually with dragon-blue glazed tiles, the blue representing vegetation, and the "element" of wood and the tree). They were supported by the post, beam and bracket construction; the wall acted solely as a screen – it had no structural function whatever. Here is a fundamental difference between the architectures of East and West. In the East, moreover, the wall never meets the underside of the eaves; this means that no practical obstacles prevent its being used to manipulate space freely and easily. Both in houses and in temples, the courtyard plan was employed, reflecting the teaching of the five elements, but without the sixth side since it is open to the sky. The number of courtyards determined status, as did the position of a house in the *fang* or neighborhood: houses with one or two courtyards opened into side streets; the more magnificent opened into main thoroughfares.

Cities were constructed of groups of *fang*, related to street-planning and to the rectangular city wall, which were again directly related to the cardinal points of the universe. Cosmic principles thus created a simple guide for the plan of a town. The spread of Buddhism from India in the 3rd century AD strengthened Chinese beliefs in such principles to the extent that structural considerations took second place. This may well be why temples were seldom grand, but followed the house pattern round courtyards (one notable exception to this is the circular Temple of Heaven, Peking, AD 1420, with its triple-tier roof).

The plan of a city was a dramatization of the house plan. With the house, there was no facade facing your approach. Instead, the succession of courtyards and rooms through which you passed presented a composite picture; time was essential to the creation of the picture, the effect of which was rather like the drop-scenes of a theater or peep-show. In China, man organized the space around him, piece by piece, in order to organize progressively his country and universe. Only from an inner calm could man discover and shape calm surroundings.

So, within the overall law of the cosmic cross that governed planning, the plan of the city was established in an orderly manner. In the center of a city was the largest houseyard complex, occupied by the emperor, who dominated the walled city as he dominated the nation. The plan of the city begins in the center; as in the house, the owner begins from the center, the guest or stranger from the gate to the street.

In Peking, which served as the imperial capital city for 500 years and whose buildings were modified continuously but without changing its original appearance, there is a central group of ceremonial halls, known as the San-Tien, where the roof shapes indicate the crossing of the axes. From this point outwards is a succession of rectangular courtyards. The palace-city is twice enclosed by city walls: first

Imperial Palace, Peking. Part of the San-Tien central group of halls. Roof shapes indicate crossings of the cosmic axes on which the city is organized

there is the wall to the Forbidden City (forbidden, that is, to all but the emperor and his family), with its corner towers; beyond this mile-long rectangle the Imperial City and the rest of the "inner city" is surrounded by a high protective wall. But the emperor dominated the *entire* nation, defined far beyond the city walls of Peking by the Great Wall of China, outside which were the barbarians – just as the man outside the gate was a stranger. Thus the architecture of the city and the palace reflects the social order of China.

THE DEVELOPMENT OF THE STYLE

The chief differences between the Chinese and Japanese styles of architecture emerge from the Chinese preoccupation with man and the Japanese preoccupation with nature and man. Chinese design evolved in a two-dimensional manner, as in the Han tile, like a drawing made without the aid of perspective; Japanese design was conceived in depth with the aid of nature. Since the development of Chinese architecture was so slow over centuries that the style appears static, a way of understanding it best lies in a single example of secular design, the house plan.

The Chinese houseyard plan is an illustration of two influences at work – one climatic, the other connected with privacy. Parts of the house, sometimes separate blocks, were influenced by the principles of cosmic orientation and the ordered movements of man in space. The space around the building was as important as the building itself. There was a succession of spaces, and preparations for these spaces, used to give order to man's immediate surroundings. These spaces begin with the entrance courtyard – which may be the only courtyard – lying between the wall to the street and the eaves of the house. This wall was merely a visual barrier; beyond it the usual street sounds could be heard, wafting over with scent of flowering trees and the buzz of voices. But when the wall is considered in conjunction with the special gateway, with its pitched, tiled roof, and with the huge, spreading eaves supported by the complex, shadowy, branching network of brackets hovering over the darkened interior, the space between had tremendous presence as a preparation for entering the building. The space under the eaves shaded the eyes and was partially enclosed. Inside was the central room or hall, known as the *ming* (meaning "bright"); this connected the porch with the inner "dark" rooms, and is another intermediate space before the total privacy of the inner rooms, found to the left or right of it.

CHINESE ETIQUETTE AND ARCHITECTURE
This plan set the stage for the drama of Chinese etiquette. A distinction is made between respect and intimacy, the guest and the owner, the longitudinal division of the house between east and west, and, in the idealized plan, between front and rear. In fact the plan followed the principle of the cosmic cross. The guest is persuaded to enter by the owner; this takes time, an important element in the construction of the composition; time is memory, a vital link with ancestor worship. The two then separate: the host takes the eastern steps on the right, and the guest turns left to take the western steps. In climbing the steps, the guest follows his host's moves, observing longitudinal symmetry, the guest raising his right foot as his host raises his left. Movement in space was planned to this precise degree. Raised terraces dictate the path; the invitation of staircases – and the taboo of forbidden corners – is stated rigidly. In houses with a number of courts, however, these rules of etiquette were waived, the ritual only beginning when the inner court was reached; it would have been too time-consuming repeated at every gateway, although the passing of each represented a further penetration of the owner's privacy.

So the Chinese doorway was much more than an opening, which is why its position in the wall was accentuated by a large roof; the roof gave it dignity. In ancient times the Chinese would have been trained from childhood to be in the right place at the right time, and to follow the right path – throughout life.

But this is still the square world – the Chinese term for the house or the city. Nature is represented by circular forms; where the square is placed inside the circle, as illustrated by the plan of Ming T'ang Piyung, Sian (early 1st century AD), the space between is called "between heaven and man" (*t'ien-jen-chih-chi*). This was the garden – where man assumed an idealized role, to think on matters of eternity. So, while man was trying to organize his world of straight lines and right angles, in the garden he could glimpse the larger, complicated order of nature. In the Chinese world, architecture and landscape were separate; architecture was processional and finite; it was symmetrical and its rigidity prevented development. The garden was on the way to heaven, but in no sense an element in a total architectural composition.

JAPANESE FLEXIBILITY
Copying Chinese principles of construction, the Japanese took things further, recognizing that structure could have a more active part in the regulation of space. They introduced a strict module which gained great flexibility in planning. We find familiar characteristics – enormous roofs in single, double or triple tiers, the immense intricacy of the bracket (seen at its finest in the Great Buddha Hall of the Todaiji, Nara, AD 745, the largest wooden building under one roof in the world), the turned-up eaves (Kongosanmai in Tahoto Pagoda, Wakayama Prefecture, 13th century), and the delicate rice paper screens and fretwork panels melting into darkness above the stone or brick podium.

The profiles are like the Chinese, and some of the materials are the same. But there are considerable and sometimes subtle differences. Japanese architecture already had its own traditions. Most important was the Shinto religion, the simple faith that gods and people, birds and animals, and everything in nature had the same father, and looked after each other's interests. Life at all levels was equal; hence a respect for nature that is more evident than in traditional Chinese architecture. There is no applied color in traditional Japanese architecture; the builders relied on the natural colors of their materials – wood, thatch, tiles, rice paper.

Great Buddha Hall, Todaiji, Nara (AD 745). The largest wooden building under one roof in the world, hiding a fretwork forest of brackets under its eaves

The Katsura Palace, Kyoto

0   50 feet

0   10   20 metres

Built in the first half of the 17th century, the Imperial Palace of Katsura reflects the zenith of Japanese architecture. Garden design flourished in the Heian period (9th-12th centuries), superseding the symmetrical basis of Chinese styles, and Katsura derives much from the teahouse architecture of the 16th century.

As an aristocratic house, Katsura should follow absolutely the kiwari method, which was based on a module – the length of span between posts measured from the center of each post – which determined the proportions of connecting beams, rafters, lintels and other visible parts of the frame. (See cutaway portion of the illustration for construction in the first room of the Old Shoin.) The module was controlled by the structural limitations of timber but the actual proportions were almost entirely based on aesthetic preferences.

At the same time, the disciplines of Zen Buddhism have refined the building so that it represents the height of simplicity and restraint, the harmony of man and nature. The post-and-bracket is reduced to light but emphatic rectangular geometry.

Natural materials – plain wood, paper, straw mats – are used, in an asymmetrical plan in which flexibility is provided by the sliding screens; through verandahs and panel openings the airy spaces of the interior are intimately connected with the landscape outside, a beautiful and subtle arrangement of rocks, pebbles, plants and water.

Students of Japanese literature can find many allusions to traditional poetry in the Katsura Palace. Passages in the 11th-century Tale of Genji and other poems may have been taken as sources for the design and can be read as descriptions of the garden and the setting.

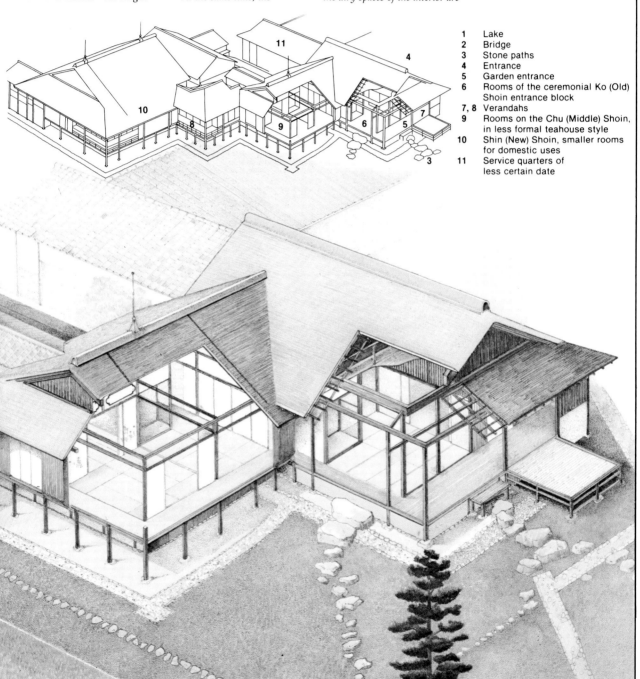

1   Lake
2   Bridge
3   Stone paths
4   Entrance
5   Garden entrance
6   Rooms of the ceremonial Ko (Old) Shoin entrance block
7, 8 Verandahs
9   Rooms on the Chu (Middle) Shoin, in less formal teahouse style
10 Shin (New) Shoin, smaller rooms for domestic uses
11 Service quarters of less certain date

Pagoda of the Toji Temple, Kyoto. The enormous many-tiered roofs and immensely intricate brackets are copied from Chinese tradition

During the middle and late Heian period (898–1185), after Buddhism had spread to Japan from the mainland, and the elaborate style of *shinden-zukuri* was being developed by the aristocracy in their mansions, houses were planned as rectangular structures connected by long corridors flexible enough to follow the contours of the ground, and to encourage garden design. There would be a carefully conceived landscape on the south side of the house, a pond or small lake with an island (like the pictures on willow-pattern cups and saucers), and the main hall, the *shinden*, was surrounded by an open verandah (a feature never seen in China). Various kinds of movable partitions, dividing internal space, suggested future subdivisions of sliding paper screens.

Symmetry, the characteristic of the intellectual Chinese plan, diminished; instead there developed an asymmetrical planning in harmony with nature, one of the characteristics of the great period of Japanese architecture in the 15th century, leading to the teahouse era of the 16th century, when the Japanese style once more became restful and spiritual. Simplicity and naturalness approximated to a state of grace, an attitude with origins in the Buddhist faith, which preaches the transience of life.

THE KATSURA PALACE, KYOTO

The Imperial Palace of Katsura, Kyoto (1590–1636) reflecting the zenith of Japanese architecture, reflects the harmonies discovered between building, landscape, and materials, and the infinite possibilities of asymmetry and flexibility. This extraordinary building also reflects the disciplines of Zen Buddhism, which arrived in Japan during the 13th century: simplicity, restraint, and the elimination of all unnecessary detail. These disciplines led to the common language of symbolism between man and nature, to tastes that cost nothing and were enjoyed collectively, and to the Japanese use of space as a physical expression of such tastes.

At Katsura, the symmetrical plan of earlier times has vanished. The structural module, decisive in repetition and unadorned with bracket detail, tiptoes over the garden and between trees, forming courtyards and verandahs with views over the carefully planned lake. As in art, the Japanese love of nature is followed in the architecture; natural color, texture, and the firm structural module unify various rhythms, sensations, and shapes into a single composition. Zen's affirmation of the reality of immediate experience – such as a momentary pattern made by foam on a river – as indivisible from the present (which is infinite) is fully confirmed in the space of Katsura Palace. The architecture clarifies the individual's relationship with nature, by its rhythmic extension from the near and definite to the distant and indefinable. Katsura is the finest existing example of visual harmony in Japanese architecture.

Tofukuji Temple Garden, Kyoto. The Japanese took preoccupation with order a step further; study of the garden led to an understanding of the more complex order of Nature

Torii of Itsukushima Shrine, Miyajima. Blades of sculpture in wood rise reed-like out of the water

Daikakuji Temple interior, Kyoto. The paper screen is rolled up to reveal a space enclosed by a wall painting. Such was the respect for nature, that the wood-grain formed part of the painting

THE JAPANESE AND ASYMMETRY

The unique contribution of Japanese architecture, the asymmetrical order, makes certain demands on the imagination; it leaves gaps which have to be filled or completed by human participation, and means that the building plan and structure can adapt to the random order of landscape. It recognizes that the essence of life is growth and change, and that architecture must make allowances for both; asymmetrical order is, of course, infinitely extendable. This larger order, which the Chinese searched for in their gardens, requires a structural framework which can accept the variations of functional requirements which make asymmetrical patterns, and allow their extension, while simultaneously relating such patterns and extensions back to the structure and smallest detail. This discipline provides the architectural order. Materials are valued for their natural shapes, properties, patterns, colors and textures; effects are accomplished by simple contrasts, and by relationships between the inherent qualities of the materials. The pervasive unity is increased by the harmony of color and textures originating in the compatibility of natural materials – the insistence on natural finish established the continuity of pattern-making from nature to architecture.

A long history of contact with nature developed a profound respect for natural forms in the Japanese, and it was in nature that the largest asymmetrical order was discovered. A simple structure provided the basis for evolving forms, and led to the close connection between construction and architectural treatment. Uprights were visible both inside and outside, and as skill increased – in, for example, the Ise Shrine building – multiple forces were resolved into their horizontal and vertical components, to create the basic rectangular geometry of post-and-beam construction. The module of this construction – the distance between columns taken from center to center of the posts, or uprights – was determined by the dimensions of the rectangular plans of the different parts of the building. Particularly in houses, this was determined by the size of the tatami straw mats, which covered the boarded floors, each 6 ft (2 m) by 3 ft (1 m) and at least 2 in (5 cm) thick, representing the minimum sleeping area for one person. Thus the module reflects the space occupied by one person. In Japanese design, the shape of the house was determined by the number and arrangement of mats: the flexibility lies in the different ways in which rooms can be used. None of the matted rooms has any exclusive purpose – sleeping, worship, living – and each can at any time be put to another use by removing or sliding of walls.

Thus Japanese design introduced standardization firmly tied to the scale of the individual. The influence of Japanese architecture – both its flexibility and its standardization – remained limited to the eastern hemisphere until the 20th century. Its special contribution was to demonstrate how space can be used economically with cheap construction. Of all the lessons that may be learnt from it, the most relevant to architecture today is flexibility. Only a really flexible outlook can meet the problems of an increasingly fast-moving world.

CHAPTER 13

Georgian

Above: The Paragon, Bath. Ingenious planning in terraces where under-pavement cellars connect directly with road level, lifting pedestrians out of harm's way

Below: Wilton House, south front (from c. 1632). The south facade of a square in plan; window proportions also derived from the square

The 18th century was an era of harmony in the arts – in architecture, music, painting, and pottery; the resultant calm is plainly seen in contemporary English architecture – Georgian. One is inclined to think of the Georgian style as domestic – terraces of brick or stone houses, sometimes four stories high, sometimes two or three; 18th-century architects saw complete neighborhoods within a human scale. Never before had all the details of a town or city – both large and small, from government buildings to window ironwork – been so designed that the whole was greater than the sum of its parts.

The Georgian style abandoned the grandiose building and dramatic vistas with which the Renaissance and Baroque are associated – the cathedrals, palaces, and vast symmetrical compositions reflecting the aspirations of great patrons of the church, government, or aristocracy. Instead the style focused on the neighborhood or town, on making elements display an equal status – not more, not less than each other; the Horse Guards building in Whitehall, London (1758), for example, was conceived on a scale that suited Inigo Jones' Banqueting House opposite (1619–22). The Georgians saw Classical order as a background to community life, so adding to architecture something which was specifically their own.

The secret of this architecture lay in its manifestation of a balanced view of life. People were deserting the country for the town; this style, with its orderly arrangement, provided a commonsense and beautiful architectural solution; the great Classical ideas, evolved over centuries, were scaled down to meet the day-to-day needs of living, and, significantly, the landscape was introduced into the city. After Michelangelo's St Peter's, Rome, European architecture took two distinct routes, one following Bernini's Baroque, the other following Palladio's much sparer forms. Palladio continued with a Grecian simplicity that had a mathematical order and domestic scale applicable to both farmhouse and large villa. In addition, he explored relationships between architecture and the landscape, eliminated all unnecessary decoration, and stressed the function of a building.

THE INFLUENCE OF INIGO JONES

This disciplined spirit of simplicity passed into English architecture via Inigo Jones (1573–1652), and formed the basis of the 18th-century style. But the Georgian style has a distinctive *Englishness* inherited from both the Englishman's love of his garden (best seen at country houses) and the slowly evolving excellence of traditional craftsmanship. Outside influences were gradually absorbed into the traditional system; we see this process happening in the work of Inigo Jones at the Queen's House, Greenwich (1616–35), St Paul's Covent Garden, London, (1631–3, the one surviving side of London's first square), and notably also in the Banqueting House, Whitehall, and at Wilton House, Wiltshire (from c. 1632), both of which made use of Palladio's double cube. We can see the same process in the work of Sir Christopher Wren who, while inspired by English traditions, took note of Classical lessons from abroad, particularly those relating to order and firm form.

The Great Fire of London in 1666, a catastrophic conflagration, created the crisis which stimulated the standardized, component-built style we so much treasure today. A row of houses was now for the first time seen as a single composition, where the center house had greater height and importance than those on either side. Stone mullions were replaced by thin, wooden window divisions; the frame was set back from the brick face, to prevent flame-spread; cornices diminished in importance; the basement was invented (to get round regulations imposing a maximum of four stories above street level); brick superseded stone whenever economic; and pilasters introduced a sub-Palladian theme.

Town planning was simplified; a district could be comprehended in large chunks, and confused, haphazard collections of individual houses became a thing of the past. By the end of the 17th century this new and sophisticated style of domestic architecture was spreading all over London. It could have fallen into the hands of the property speculators but for the intervention of a group of ardent followers of Inigo Jones and Palladio – namely, Colen Campbell, Lord Burlington, and William Kent, the designer of the Horse Guards building, who published a book on Inigo Jones in 1727. It was this group who restored space and elegance to architecture, and firmly established once more the style of Palladio and Jones. We see this from their work – Mereworth Castle, Kent (Campbell 1722–5), Burlington House, London (Burlington, with Campbell 1719), and Kent's additions to Rousham Park, Oxfordshire. The preferred material of the Georgian style was brick (cheaper to make, easier

Mereworth Castle. Campbell's homage to Palladio's Villa Rotunda fails to make the strong links with landscape seen in the original, but shows the extent of the Palladian influence. The central hall shows how the simplicity of the original is lost

to build, than stone). The favorite in London was hard "stock" for all outer walls, although some public buildings were built of Portland stone, while internal walls and partitions were made of a very cheap brick made of a mixture of clay and ash. Stone was also widely used in various parts of the country – Bath stone across the country from Somerset to Lincoln; gritstone in Yorkshire, so hard and difficult to cut that it produced a very plain architecture; granite in Cornwall and Scotland; slate in Wales. Brick of various colors was largely limited to Wales and to southern and eastern England. Thus differences of character in the Georgian style emerge. Roof structures were also domestic in scale: timber rafters for houses, and wooden trusses for the larger spans in churches and theaters.

The Royal Crescent, Bath

John Wood's designs for Bath were drawn from three sources: his interest in archaeology, his belief in the principles of Palladian architecture, and the current fashion in architecture, particularly as practiced by Colen Campbell and James Gibbs.

As Bath was originally a Roman spa, Wood's idea to introduce Roman forms into his planning seemed entirely in keeping with the history of the city. Of course Roman streets and domestic architecture did not take this form. Wood borrowed the circus and the crescent from the amphitheaters and theaters of Rome. The square was an Italian idea developed in France and England during the 17th century.

Wood's housing was for the well-to-do people of Bath. His ambitious planning (and the patronage of Beau Nash) made Bath the most fashionable resort of the 18th century. Wood himself was not concerned with the actual building, merely insisting that the houses be built with facades to his design.

Queen Square (left) was begun in 1729, the Circus in 1754, and the Royal Crescent, designed by his son (also John), begun in 1767 after the father's death. The Royal Crescent is a terrace of 30 houses joined in

one palatial facade in which the detail of individual dwellings is unified in the shape of the Crescent, by the regular sequence of Ionic columns and the horizontals of the column plinth and the balustrade parapet. The interior of Number One has been restored (see cutaway).

The fine detailing of glazing bars, fanlights, front doors and metalwork was part of the grammar of 17th- and 18th-century architecture in England. Not only did these details ornament the facade, they were also necessary to the function of the building.

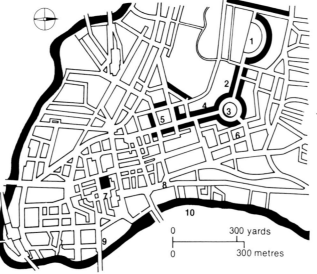

The plan of Bath. Buildings 1-6 are by the Woods, father and son.
1   Royal Crescent
2   Brock Street
3   The Circus
4   Gay Street
5   Queen Square
6   Assembly Rooms
7   Pump Room and Roman Baths
8   High Street
9   North Parade
10 River Avon

0   300 yards
0   300 metres

ROYAL CRESCENT, BATH

The Acropolis in Athens was a great architectural conception; at Bath we find a less great conception – but nonetheless remarkable – in the combined plans and forms of Queen Square, the Circus, Royal Crescent, and connecting streets. At Bath, the entire vision was the work of a father and son – John Wood, the elder (1704–54) and John Wood, the younger (1728–81). Both had short lives, but between them what they accomplished was vast; since the father's work was continued by his son one might well think that the father lived twice.

Bath became fashionable in the 1700s, leading to its orderly development through the 18th and 19th centuries in squares, crescents and streets, all derived from the Classical ideas of the Woods. John Wood, the elder, was born in Yorkshire, and had from early years a great interest in Bath. In his 20s he had an idea for the plan of the town, and, when this was accepted, he settled there in 1728. The genius of Wood's plan turns on his imaginative choice of a site for the center of Bath; it started low and finished at a higher level, with a magnificent hillside view across the River Avon. All the more extraordinary, he picked the site while he was still in Yorkshire, plainly recognizing that the center of a town needs space. First, there is Queen Square, only the third to be built in England, with such a grand north side that Wood might have been designing a palace; then there is the innovatory Circus, a Roman amphitheater scaled down to domestic size; and finally, the greatest surprise of all, the Royal Crescent: the space framed by square, circus and streets is suddenly released with the view over the river and countryside. Each form has common elements with the next: the square and circus both control space, and the crescent is semi-elliptical, the circus acting as the focus of the composition. So powerful is Wood's architectural statement that it guided all other developments in Bath for the next hundred years.

The building of Queen Square began in 1729, only a year after Wood's arrival, and was finished seven years later. The Circus was begun in 1754, just before Wood's death, and Royal Crescent, designed by his son, in 1767. The Woods, of course, also designed many of the surrounding streets – the Parades, Brock Street, Wood Street, Gay Street, and others. Later squares and crescents, such as St James's Square, Lansdowne and Norfolk Crescents, picked up where the Woods left off. Various architects were involved, and every street is a work of art. Bath was, until recently, the most beautiful of English cities. Yet, despite dramatic protests, great damage has been done to the city by 20th-century architects and planners. Do

not, therefore, be disappointed to find that Bath is no longer the lovely vision the Woods intended. The center has been cut back to a museum piece. In this world, we are perhaps lucky still to have this.

DEVELOPMENT OF THE STYLE

In the Georgian period it seemed that architects, builders, and craftsmen could not put a foot wrong. These people seem to have hit a golden streak, or broken some complicated aesthetic code which led to the discovery of a new architectural language. The real secret of their success, however, simply lies in what Palladio would have called an orderly relation of parts, a formula which applies to the design of a neighborhood as much as to that of a single building. Thus, let us say, a church must relate to streets around it; the church must provide a center of interest, but not so as to dominate surrounding streets and detract from them. In other words, the 18th-century architect was determined to make a picture where all the parts collaborated to produce a perfect composition. He saw that a relationship must be forged not only between different kinds of buildings but also between architecture and landscape.

BEGINNINGS OF LANDSCAPE DESIGN

The design of landscape paralleled the design of buildings. Buildings require the qualities of nature to add color and movement, to soften the edges of stone or brick. In the 18th-century conception, the country and the architecture met in the garden. We get one of the first glimpses of the great developments in landscape design to come at Wilton House, Wiltshire, a square building set down as an ornament in a park. The next glimpse is at Rousham where William Kent added to the 17th-century house a pair of wings and stables, which might almost have been the work of Palladio himself; he also designed the garden. Here was the breakthrough: gone is the fussy, geometric European garden plan, laid like pretentious carpets outside the front doors of so many stately homes. Instead the country is allowed to run up to the windows along with, so to speak, the cows and sheep. After Rousham came Stowe, Buckinghamshire, where Kent discovered the great landscape gardener, Lancelot "Capability" Brown, and thereby changed the face of English estates. Stowe was a masterpiece, and so was every garden Brown undertook – Audley End, Essex; the Cambridge Backs; Blenheim Park, Oxfordshire, and scores more.

The freedom Kent and Brown brought to landscape design was introduced to the town: lawns round stately homes and city squares. The square was an

In "Capability" Brown's masterpiece of landscaping at Blenheim Park (1760), the illusion of a broad river was created mainly by damming a spring, and the "banks" were bordered with meadows and clumps of trees, the whole surrounded by woodlands

English innovation where country and the town met, and a balance with nature, the goal of Georgian town planning, was achieved. A softening of line and edges is essential in a static urban scene, as is the movement of leaves and shadow, and change of color; the square seems the ideal, and the most beautiful, answer. Trees and bushes were planted thickly round the perimeter, and, in summer, the green center became a secluded breathing space amidst a dense city. The surrounding terraces can hardly be seen for foliage, while their windows have the advantage of overlooking trees which also shade rooms from heat and glare. In winter, when the leaves have fallen and light is poorer, shade is not required: the terraces have a view of space.

The square led to another English speciality – the park: supremely John Nash and Humphry Repton's masterpiece, Regent's Park, London (1811–35). This relating of architecture to nature was echoed in the factors which regulated building-heights in a town. For example, a square normally has four stories, an important street has three, a lane (like the now fashionable mews) has two. Similarly a town has a park, a district has a square or two, a street has its trees and a house has its garden. These simple rules produced a green thread connecting various parts of a town or city, and connecting the town or city with the country. Balance was accomplished. Again, there is no more magnificent example than the plan of Bath: in addition to the square, we have the crescent and circus, their curved forms going further towards a union with nature.

Sussex Place, Regent's Park, London (1811-35). One of John Nash's terraces designed for the aristocracy round a park. The colonnade subordinates the individual house to the city scale

THE GENIUS OF ROBERT ADAM

The Georgian era was like a little Renaissance. The 18th century was full of brilliant men who put Classical forms to work on a domestic scale; there is no question that the English have a remarkable talent in adopting the grand ideas of others in a universally acceptable manner. Just when Palladian inspiration was losing its originality, and declining into textbook solutions – with architects thoughtlessly facing their houses north, as the Italians did, rather than south to suit a cooler climate – another great figure appeared to save the day: Robert Adam (1728–92). Like Palladio, he gave the name to a style – Adam ceilings, Adam fireplaces, Adam decoration. He leapt to prominence because he had an original mind, and believed absolutely in originality. When he went to Italy, he did personal research, made his own drawings and returned with his own conclusions. His subsequent influence on architecture, limited, unfortunately, by absence of large commissions, lay in his originality of outlook and his lightness of touch. He restored delicacy to design: beautiful detail, tiny moldings, freedom of line and color. The Palladian severity had gone, yet not the Classical disciplines – as we see at Syon House (c. 1760–69, from a plan by Inigo Jones), Osterley Park (1761–80), the Adelphi (1768–72), Kenwood House (1767–9), all in London; his castles (notably, Culzean, Scotland, 1777–90); and his last great work, New Edinburgh (designed 1791). By attacking the Palladian establishment, and by loosening the grip of academics such as Sir William Chambers, architect to Somerset House (1776–86), Adam did more for Georgian architecture than anyone since William Kent and John Wood, the elder; his influence gave the style the delicacy and mellow beauty one associates with that great period.

The Georgian style spread everywhere. In Britain, it traveled from London to York, Norwich, Bristol, Derby, Nottingham, Edinburgh, not to mention Bath and elsewhere; it spread to the British colonies, among them North America, where it was directly copied in the Federal architecture of the late 18th century, and even to Norway, where it was copied in vertical boarding. It is no surprise to find a perfect Georgian port in Tasmania, backed up by white-painted bow-fronted Regency terraces as good as any to be seen in Brighton, Sussex.

Osterley Park, Middlesex (1761-80), by Robert Adam. The portico directs attention to the entrance courtyard, but its use as a colonnade in addition is unique. The Tapestry Room ceiling (below) shows Adam's delicate interpretation of Classical disciplines

CHAPTER 14

American Colonial

Mention of the American Colonial style conjures up a picture of 18th-century East Coast Americans under wide-brimmed hats sipping long, cool drinks in the shade of the verandahs of white, weatherboarded houses with shallow-pitched roofs and deep eaves. Examples of this white style of architecture are to be found spread over thousands of miles, through Maine, New Hampshire, Vermont, Massachusetts, Connecticut, New York, down into New Jersey, Virginia, North and South Carolina, and Georgia. It was as unique as it was pure, perfect, and relaxed: window divisions as thin as pencil lines, bricks exactly laid, fanlights delicately designed, pilasters as sharp as clear sunlight. Everything the style touched – whether house, barn, church, warehouse, mill, or public building – was left immaculate; the most fastidious architect's sensibility, the most precise carpenter's plane had passed over it.

But the American style also has much to do with a hardworking age when people used their money to build homes of great quality, to bring up children in secure surroundings, and to interest themselves in beautiful things such as good craftsmanship and furniture.

The origins of this beautiful style are simple enough. It was in effect a cross between the log cabin brought to Delaware by 17th-century Swedish settlers and the classical discipline of the English Georgian style, introduced 100 years or so later. In 1630 English settlers were still groping with medieval forms, with oak beams, plaster, wattle, and thatch. But the moment the first sawmill came into operation, in 1649, the weatherboard style developed rapidly, from cottage to house architecture by the end of the 17th century. It evolved parallel with Georgian architecture in England, and was a free interpretation of its English counterpart. The attachment of shutters, verandahs, and balconies, together with curious variations of size – one, two, or three stories – gave the style a strong horizontal emphasis, and a great generosity and openness. An individuality, often noticeable from house to house, tied the style to the scale of the street, distinguishing it markedly from English Georgian

Above: church at Melvin, New Hampshire. The form of an English church, clothed in white dress

Below: Arcadian House, Baton Rouge, Louisiana. The elements of the Colonial style: brick, boarding, the porch and its posts

Monticello, Charlottesville, Virginia

Monticello is an early building of the American Classical Revival. It was built at a time when in England and France architects were concerned with antiquity and primary sources. Jefferson looked back to Palladio in a country which already had many 18th-century buildings drawn from James Gibbs and the English Palladians.

Monticello is not a palace but a fairly small country house. Building started in 1770 on a Greek-cross plan with Palladian porticos to east (two stories) and west. After Jefferson's five years as minister to France, where he admired the building of P. Rousseau's Hôtel de Salm in Paris, the house was remodeled (1795–1808) with side extensions containing rooms of a variety of shapes (all cleverly opening onto the central hall or corridors). A central dome was added, and the general plan of

the house, with stairs leading to the enclosed loggias to north and south which echo the main porticos (both now single-story), recalls the influential Villa Rotunda of Palladio. The plan (right) shows the original building in solid tones.

At the same time the building is unmistakably American. The combination of brick and crisp white-painted woodwork, and the horizontal emphasis of shutters, and balconies opening onto the garden, make it an original, imaginative and unacademic heir to European traditions.

Many details testify to Jefferson's design ingenuity. Double doors inside open together, when just one door is moved, through an under-floor arrangement of pulleys. All the chief building materials were prepared on the estate itself: stone, bricks, wood, even nails.

Jefferson also planned an elaborate landscape garden decorated with Greek, Gothic and Chinese (as in the trellis fencing) structures. He seems to have been influenced by the English Romantic garden. He made plans for enlarging the grounds at the same time as he was remodeling the house, and the range of service buildings, including the kitchen, is an

important part of the original design for living. It was accommodated beneath the L-shaped "terrace walks" to north and south.

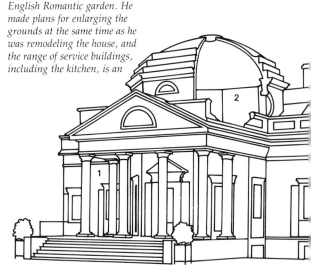

1 Doric west portico opening
   onto Parlour
2 Wooden dome, and octagonal
   Dome Room
3 Chinese trellis railing
4 Basement extending to service
   rooms below terraces
5 Original south wing extended:
   Jefferson's bedroom, library
   suite, and enclosed arched loggia
6 First-floor window disguised
   to give illusion of single story
7 Hall opening onto east portico

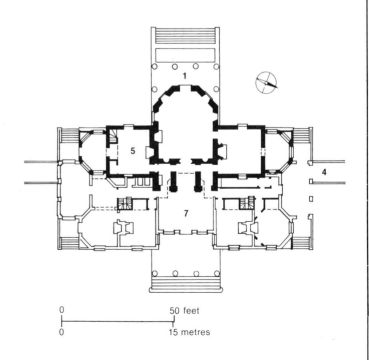

0   50 feet
0   15 metres

Old Colony House, Newport, Rhode Island (1739). A derivative of Sir Christopher Wren's domestic style, but the eccentricity of Richard Munday's interpretation shows in the pediment

which had meanwhile developed to a scale to embrace a whole city.

Many examples of this delightful spacious style have, regrettably, been demolished; but there is much of it still to be seen both in the New England states and further south. Besides the University of Virginia, Charlottesville (1817–26), and Georgetown, near Washington DC (laid out 1751), there are houses in Delaware such as the David Wilson Mansion (1769) and the Corbit-Sharp House (1774), and Christ Church, Philadelphia (1727–54) and the Old Colony House, Newport, Rhode Island (1739).

In the earliest buildings walls were framed in handsawn, heavy timber, with the spaces between filled with brick or stone, like half-timbering in northern Europe. Exteriors and interiors were then boarded over, the exterior with weatherboarding.

With the introduction of brick, however, timber-framing was first covered over, and then omitted altogether; weatherboarding became a facing to improve protection against damp and cold. Roofs were constructed in the customary fashion, with cedar shingles on rafters. Bricks were first imported from Britain and the Netherlands, but plenty of good brick clay was discovered in the late 17th century in Pennsylvania and New Jersey, and brick-making quickly got under way.

MONTICELLO, CHARLOTTESVILLE, VIRGINIA
Monticello was designed from c. 1769 by Thomas Jefferson (1743–1826), third president of the United States, for his own use. In this original form the house was perhaps the finest example of the Colonial style, but it was completely remodeled by Jefferson in a Palladian manner between 1796 and 1808. The building is a most original, imaginative and unacademic heir to the European Classical tradition. No wonder, then, that Monticello, together with the University of Virginia, Charlottesville (1817–26), also by Jefferson, had a huge influence on American architecture of the times.

Monticello is one of a number of great houses which took their inspiration from Palladio's Villa Rotunda (begun c. 1550). Among the others were Colen Campbell's Mereworth Castle, Kent, England (1722–5), and Chiswick House, London (1725) by Lord Burlington and William Kent. Monticello is, however, an improvement on its rivals. It was not in a valley or on flat ground, as are Mereworth and Chiswick, but on the top of a gently rounded hill, giving views in all directions and bringing it closer to the Italian original. Jefferson's first building, of 1778, was a simple Greek cross with porticos back and front; the remodeled design follows Palladio's Rotunda more closely, with porticos on all four sides, and flights of steps leading up to them.

But the second design for Monticello was not a slavish imitation of the Rotonda – as Mereworth was – another reason why Monticello is better than Mereworth or Chiswick. Although it reflects a scholarly understanding and reverence for the past, Monticello was designed to suit the present. Its plan is, in fact, a good deal more complex and functional than the Rotonda's; for example, all ground floor rooms have access either from the central hall or from corridors, and every foot of space is carefully used. Jefferson's design was exceedingly clever. The porticos were seen as tools to help simplify the complex plan, by producing an elevation with a domestic scale. The free forms of the library, study, drawing-room, tea-room, and octagonal bedroom become delightful variations within a strong symmetrical composition, governed and expressed by the presence of the porticos: and two stories appear to be one. Thus Palladio's conception – of a hill crowned with a dome – is followed, but not in such a way as to deny domestic proportions for modern requirements. A test of greatness is the degree to which the work of a genius can be absorbed by the disciple without ill effects. Monticello illustrates this form of greatness, which was Jefferson's.

DEVELOPMENT OF THE STYLE

In Georgian architecture in England, it was the combination of craftsmanship and Classical disciplines which gave the style its honesty and quality. The weatherboarding of the Colonial style underlines the same point. The white painted work produces a beautiful architecture with a startling clarity and eloquence; it is no coincidence that the great modern Swiss architect, Le Corbusier, was fascinated by the style when he was driven round East Hampton, Long Island, and shown an unspoilt Colonial village. The carpentry contributes simplicity and sharpness to the fine lines of the windows, paneled doors, fanlights and shutters, while the architect's discipline contributed the order that encouraged every aspect to excel, and not least the sense of spaciousness that the white paint introduced to facades, decorated on occasion with black-painted ironwork.

Colonial was also a flexible architecture; in town or city the substitution of brick for weatherboarding allowed variations in height or width, or in the detail of facades and levels. We see excellent examples of this in Georgetown, Washington; a number of variables can be collected to make a comprehensible whole, in a neighborhood divided into equal-sided blocks on the gridiron plan. Americans much favored this town planning form in the 18th and 19th centuries – a form which, of course, originated in Roman times.

Shaker Town, Kentucky. The Shakers' movement spread in East Coast states in the 19th century, building in the sparest Colonial style

Saratoga Springs, New York. A richer more formal Colonial house and gardens, with verandah, carved posts and white boarding

Above: Shaker Town, interior. This spartan interior is typical of the Colonial style, as is the familiar rocking chair

THE ENGLISH CONTRIBUTION

The English style represented the first breakthrough in industrial building techniques; it was an architecture of standard parts – bricks, doors, windows, fanlights, and the rest. But the Americans made adjustments to suit their own circumstances. For instance, the Americans simplified brick dimensions. Then, while the English set windows back to meet new fire regulations after the Great Fire of 1666, the Americans set them forward so that their frames followed the

Oak Alley, Vacherie (1837). A Louisiana plantation house that returns to the purity of ancient Greece; the Giant Order produces a two-story verandah that is like a double peristyle

Nottoway, White Castle, Louisiana (1859). The Giant Order here is raised on a rusticated base. This is a 64-room mansion

surface of the outside walls. Methods used for weather protection in timber-framed buildings were adopted as a *style* of building, and the precise point at which one material departed from another appeared as no more than a line – no shadows, no modulations. So, from copying the English, the American settler went on to find an indigenous style of his own, which became steadily more sophisticated during the 18th century. And then, as this neighborhood architecture spread across the East Coast area, rich people began building large Palladian villas.

In Europe, building forms contracted to meet less grand requirements, and greater economies in planning; the Georgian terrace reflected this trend. But in the United States, the reverse process occurred; people started with little and grew richer. Social needs and ambitions increased; wealthy Virginians wanted something of lasting value to show for their wealth – rather like the Florentine merchants of the 15th century. When President Jefferson designed and built Monticello he set the style for the beautiful grand houses which began to appear in the states of the East. Among the best were Oak Alley, Vacherie, Louisiana (1836); Belmont, Nashville, Tennessee (1850); Mark Anthony de Wolf House (1835 – destroyed by fire 1920), Bristol; Hillhouse (1835), New Haven; Arlington House, Virginia (1802–37). Most had porticos, most were landscaped, and stucco (a grander version of weatherboarding, with the same effect) was common. All were perfectly designed and made, down to the last door handle and brass lock. This sudden outpouring of Colonial mansions was a last glimpse of the Renaissance. But these beautiful, stylish houses led nowhere. They arrived too late. Waiting round the corner to demolish their high aesthetic ideals was the Industrial Revolution.

Nathaniel Russel House (1809). Colonial design at its most exquisite. Similar detail is found in many houses in Savannah, Georgia

CHAPTER 15

Revivals

Revival architecture could be regarded as a last-ditch fight to preserve the status quo, and to keep the technological barbarians at bay. The 19th-century was an age of extremes: imitation on the one hand, innovation on the other. This is all the more extraordinary following the balance of the 18th century.

Architectural revivals often give rise to great confusion. The 19th-century revivalist movement in Europe carried such conviction that it is sometimes difficult to decide the date of particular buildings. Some works possess so fine an air of civic pride in Second Empire richness (in France), so detailed a knowledge of Gothic structure (in England), so great a regard for Baroque space (in Austria), that one can only conceive of them as highly distinguished in their own right. Yet the essence of the age of revivals was eclecticism; we are left puzzled since the choice of a style had far more to do with an architect's personal preferences and whims, and with a fear of change, than the function of the building he had to design. And so a prestigious commission such as a town hall, church or opera house was Greek, Gothic, Romanesque, Florentine, or Baroque; but never cast iron and glass or brick – ingredients that belonged to the industrial style and were reserved for more mundane projects: warehouses, factories, and the railway stations. An important building had to be given some great style from the past if its design was to display the grandeur it deserved.

So we find Baroque at the Paris Opera (1861–75) by Charles Garnier, Gothic at the Houses of Parliament, London (1836–60), by Sir Charles Barry and A. W. N. Pugin, Classical Greek in the Parliament Building, Vienna (1873–83) by Theophil von Hansen, who also designed the Vienna Army Museum in the Venetian Byzantine style, and Rococo at the Schloss Linderhof (1870–86), by Georg von Dollman, in Bavaria.

Revivalist styles reflected the national characteristics and traditions of different countries, which is why we find Baroque predominant in central Europe, the more flamboyant features of northern Italian Renaissance architecture in France (but also a varied mixture of Roman, Romanesque, and Byzantine arches and other

Paris Opera, by Charles Garnier. This Baroque Revival piece owes much to Versailles and to the architecture of Bernini as a whole

Vienna: Parliament Building, by Theophil von Hansen. Total focus on the portico identifies this as a work of Classical temple revival

forms), and in England a battle between neo-Greek (a side-effect of Lord Burlington and Sir William Chambers' variety of Palladian purity) and neo-Gothic (a natural extension of the "picturesque" in landscape design, follies, and fashion).

The Houses of Parliament, London

The neo-Gothic Houses of Parliament (or Palace of Westminster) (1836–60) are perhaps the finest work of the "Age of Revivals." The design was by Sir Charles Barry and Augustus Pugin.

The fact that the Houses of Parliament are so obviously not a revival in plan or elevation, but merely in detail, reveals much behind the design of this

building. The planning of so much – two chambers, one for the Lords and one for the Commons, restaurants, offices, libraries and lobbies – incorporated within what appears to be one vast palace has no earlier source. The

architects have not looked back for their plan to older palaces, for the function of Westminster Palace is so completely different.
The formal plan, with its

Classical undertones, may be the work of Barry, a neo-Classical architect. The masterly town planning incorporated in the Palace is matched by the use made of the unique riverside site. The long horizontal of the Thames facade is balanced by the towers which punctuate and frame the complex with verticals accentuated by Pugin's Gothic detail.

The 19th century produced an archaeological approach to Gothic. Old buildings were measured and recorded in the same way that Classical buildings were being documented. This respect for the past is clearly demonstrated by the inclusion of the 14th-century Westminster Hall into the design.

Pugin's interest in Gothic is expressed fully in the interiors (below the Peers' Staircase). It was very much to do with accuracy and in particular with the Gothic of what he considered to be the most pure, what is now called Early English. He was not interested in the Romantic qualities of Gothic but in its suitability for use in building in England and in the importance of Gothic for church architecture.

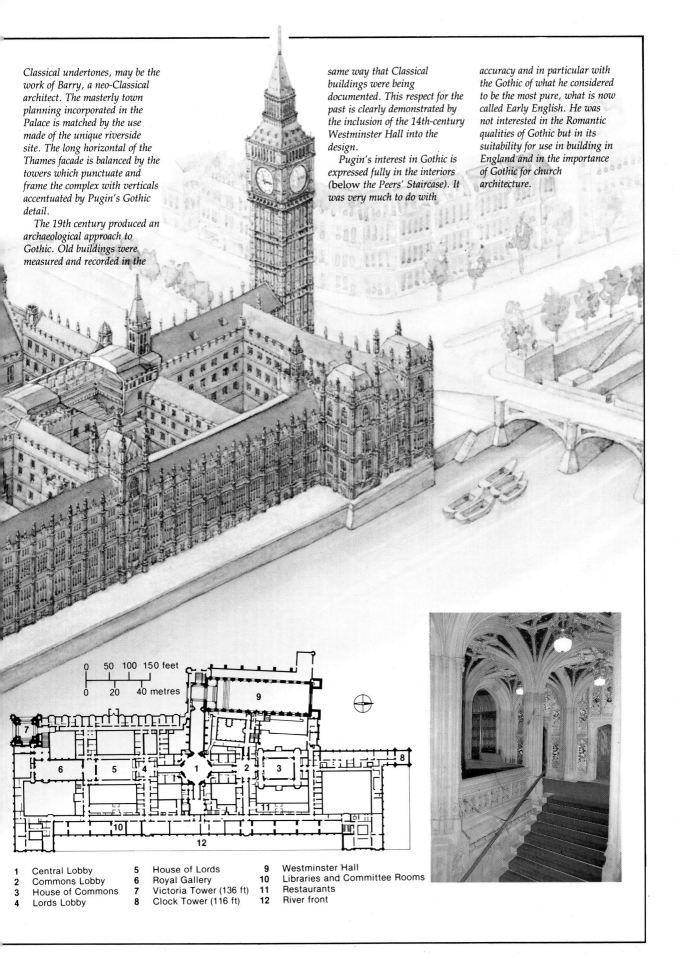

0	50	100	150 feet
0	20		40 metres

1	Central Lobby	5	House of Lords	9	Westminster Hall
2	Commons Lobby	6	Royal Gallery	10	Libraries and Committee Rooms
3	House of Commons	7	Victoria Tower (136 ft)	11	Restaurants
4	Lords Lobby	8	Clock Tower (116 ft)	12	River front

All Souls, Oxford (1715-40). Gothic originals transcended by Nicholas Hawksmoor's originality and invention

Strawberry Hill, Twickenham (from 1748). A romantic hotch-potch of styles including Gothic. Anything, it seemed, to keep the technological barbarians at bay

THE GOTHIC REVIVAL

Gothic Revival was, in fact, an English invention. The truth is that despite the powerful Classical intervention of Inigo Jones and his disciples, Gothic had never really departed from the scene – the undercurrents of Gothic reappear in Tudor forms such as Sir Christopher Wren's Tom Tower, Christ Church, Oxford (1682), and in his church spires (although these also echo the telescope forms which so interested him). Gothic also survived in the work of Nicholas Hawksmoor (see the minarets at All Souls', Oxford, 1715–40, influenced by Gothic at Magdalen), of the playwright and architect Sir John Vanbrugh, and particularly in Horace Walpole's Strawberry Hill (from 1748), and, of course, in the poetry, particularly Milton and Spenser, and other literary influences which encouraged the romanticism and informality of the landscape architecture of William Kent, Capability Brown, and Humphry Repton. Yet the Classical influence also remained strong, through the work of academics such as Sir William Chambers. Classical and Gothic strived together; in England, it was Gothic that dominated, while on much of the European continent it was the Classical theme that was supreme.

In France, too, Gothic was favored, and was associated with a growing interest in cast iron construction. In English Gothic cast iron was largely used decoratively, and then only in the High Victorian period (1850–70); the French, on the other hand, saw the obvious connections between cast iron – its slenderness, its strength, and its possibilities for shaping and reproduction of details – with Gothic forms. Thus in France Gothic became less academic, more inventive; Ste-Clotilde, Paris (1846–57) by F. C. Gau, and St-Eugène, Paris (1854–5) by L.-A. Boileau, and the work of Henri Labrouste and his associate, Eugène-Emmanuel Viollet-le-Duc, are typical examples.

THE HOUSES OF PARLIAMENT, LONDON

It is difficult to dispute that the Houses of Parliament, London, are the finest piece of revival architecture. Sir Charles Barry and Augustus Pugin won the commission in a national competition, but since Barry was a Classical architect it is probable that the main credit for design should go to Pugin, a Gothic architect. An extraordinary work of architecture that transcends style, the Parliament buildings are also a great piece of town-planning design. This focuses on three main factors: the formal plan with its Classical undertones (probably from Barry), placed so close to the Thames that the river acts as a datum for the plan; the very long low main body of the buildings; and three towers – the tall Victoria Tower at the south end, the shorter tower of the Central Hall, and at the north end the slim, tall clock tower (housing bells including "Big Ben"), which, at 316 ft (95 m), is 20 ft shorter than the Victoria Tower. So we have a balance of horizontal and vertical forms, both stressed by the thin, delicate, vertical Gothic detail.

But it is the clock tower upon which the design, both of the building and of the surrounding district, depends and focuses. A clock tower is a magnificent town-planning concept, making a superb conclusion to the sweep of Westminster Bridge, to George Street, and to the east and west views from the Embankment. With a clock on each face, the eye is inevitably drawn to the tower, to the center of government, the center of a great city. It also acts dramatically as a pivot for Parliament Square and the Parliament buildings. Here is a total conception that works on all levels, and as a meeting of Classical and Gothic, the Houses of Parliament make a perfect conclusion for the Age of Revivals.

STYLES

The Age of Revivals is usually dated 1830–70; of course, it straggled beyond these limits, but these years represent its peak, when some of the most important buildings were carried out. In England, as we have seen, the revivalist movement was beginning to gain momentum, with Strawberry Hill. From 1780 onwards James Wyatt, a Classical architect, poured out an immense amount of work of a strongly Gothic nature, culminating in the huge, romantic, and ill-fated Fonthill Abbey, Wiltshire (from 1796), which collapsed in 1807 because there were no proper foundations beneath the 278 ft (85 m) tall central tower. In the first place, the somewhat frivolous nature of Gothic Revival was a reaction against dull Classicism when the Palladian movement had run out of inspiration. This led to a counterattack from Classical disciples, and ended with a battle of styles in the 19th

century. So, while Wyatt was adding to Wilton House, Salisbury in Gothick (as it was called), George Dance, the younger, was remodeling Stratton Park, Hampshire (1806, demolished and rebuilt 1964), in Greek Revival. But Gothic was the more impressive of the two styles (as well as the most widespread), largely because the structure and openness of vaulted interiors on skeleton frameworks left room for imagination and atmospheric effects, whatever the building involved. The finest, most original examples include the Science Museum, Oxford University (1855–9) by Sir Thomas Deare and Benjamin Woodward, where, unusually, cast iron was employed for the structure; All Saints, Margaret Street, London (1849–59) by William Butterfield (modeled on 14th-century Gothic); the Town Hall, Manchester (1869–77) by Alfred Waterhouse; and St Luke's Church, Chelsea (1820–24) by James Savage (the first Gothic Revival church in London).

In France the Classical Revival was given initial encouragement by the massive replanning of Paris by Baron Georges-Eugène Haussmann (1853–68), which

All Saints, Margaret Street, London (1849-59). Despite technological developments all Gothic Revival lacks the delicacy of the original

ensured, among other things, that the city could be easily policed. This axial planning was combined with the architecture of Classicism. The Ringstrasse planning-scheme in Vienna, begun 1858, had a similar appearance, as did central Budapest and Rome, where large scale town-planning improvements were carried out in the mid-19th century.

France also had an interest in Gothic; although never as popular as in England, the French version of Gothic Revival was sparked off not by Romanticism, but by a hardheaded understanding of the use of cast iron. French preeminence in civil engineering led to important contributions throughout the century to structural design; the Library of Ste-Geneviève and Karl Friedrich Schinkel's work, notably the cast iron Kreuzberg War Memorial (1818), in Germany, where the Gothic style was regarded as having special national associations, were important revivalist influences.

Eventually, however, the Renaissance became the dominant style in France, the German states and Italy; while in Austria, a Baroque eclecticism prevailed in the later 19th century. But it was in Spain that the most original architecture suddenly appeared with Antoni Gaudí (1852–1926), whose work both anticipated and influenced Art Nouveau – itself a free form of Gothic Revival – as can be seen at his luxury apartment, Casa Milá, Barcelona (1905–10). While the French influence was dominant on the European continent, it was the British influence that went overseas – to Australia, New Zealand, India, and the United States. In America, as in Britain, the Classical movement held out for a time, and an interesting example of Roman revival is Belle Grove, near White Castle, Louisiana (1857), an extraordinary house with 75 rooms; Trinity Church, Boston (1872–7) by H. H. Richardson, and Trinity Church, New York (1841–6) by Richard Upjohn are both good examples of Gothic Revival. St John's Anglican Cathedral, Brisbane, Australia by J. L. Pearson (designed 1897, begun 1901) is a dramatic recollection of English Perpendicular.

Top: Budapest. Axial city planning in Classical Revival as in Rome, Vienna, Paris. Motorway style today has a similar effect

Center: Mormon Temple, Salt Lake City, Utah (1853-83, Truman O. Angel). Invention carries this vigorous design beyond pure imitation

Below: Kreuzberg Memorial, Berlin (1818), by Schinkel. Pure Gothic Revival, in cast iron, became standard for this type of edifice

CHAPTER 16

The Industrial Style

It was Britain – the first industrial nation – that pioneered the industrial style of architecture. With the Industrial Revolution – the age of iron and steel – came the possibilities of new building materials, and a demand for new and daring solutions to structural problems. First iron, and then after 1860 steel, gave the possibility of spanning wider distances, and building higher than ever before. Using glass with iron and steel, the engineers could make entire walls or roofs.

Just a few years after Horace Walpole put the finishing touches to a Gothic gallery at Strawberry Hill in 1763, Abraham Darby designed the world's first cast iron bridge, across the River Severn, at Coalbrookdale (1771 – 81).

Astonishingly the great period of the industrial style ran parallel with the revivalist movements. But while men of taste were admiring Strawberry Hill, Darby's bridge passed virtually unnoticed. Contemporary aesthetes probably never noticed anything so utilitarian as Thomas Telford's warehouses at St Katherine's Docks, London (1825), where the weighty brick structures were supported on cast iron Doric columns with enormous diameters.

In most architecture of the time, considerable trouble was taken to cover up the structure. But the industrial

Abraham Darby's bridge at Coalbrookdale, Shropshire, the first iron bridge in the world. From a print published in 1806

The Iron Bridge at Colebrook Dale.

Print.d Mar.1,1809, for Richard Phillips, 6, New Bridge St. Blackfriars.

Top left: cast iron and brick in the warehouses at St Katherine's Dock, London, designed by Thomas Telford (1825)

Top right: the corn mill built by F. E. Stevens at Sherdlow in 1780 on the then newly completed Trent Canal

Above: the boatstore in the former Naval Dockyard at Sheerness, Kent (G. T. Greene, 1858–61)

style was concerned solely with structure: the structure *was* the facade – as in an early example by F. E. Stevens of a corn mill at Sherdlow, Burton-on-Trent (1780). Structure and Georgian influence apart, this utilitarian architecture was constructed from standard components such as windows, doors, columns and beams – all designed without ornamentation and cheaply produced by machine. Buildings in the industrial style were refreshingly functional. They have a healthy disregard for any attempt to keep up architectural appearances; there are no delusions of grandeur about the repetitive windows of the Sheerness Naval Dockyard buildings of the 1850s or of Pyemore Mill, near

Bridport, Dorset (about 1800), or of the door and window panels of the Portsmouth Naval Dockyard fire station (1879). Industrial expansion stimulated the rapid construction of simple shells. It is this unpretentious approach to architecture, and the utilitarian solution of problems in building design, which distinguishes the industrial style and makes it so satisfying.

THE ENGINEER'S CONTRIBUTION

For us today the most striking examples of the industrial style lie in the field of engineering, characterized by immense economy of structure and materials. The bridges were an extraordinary combination of daring and simplicity; that great bridge and waterway engineer, Thomas Telford, designed his first bridge over the River Severn in 1795–6. Called the Buildwas Bridge, it was inspired by Coalbrookdale; although a longer span, it used less than half the tonnage of iron. Telford designed a number of spectacular bridges of which the Waterloo Bridge at Bettws-y-Coed, Wales (1815) was perhaps the most beautiful and the Menai Straits Suspension Bridge (1819–24) the most significant. Most remarkable, the Clifton Suspension Bridge, Bristol, by Isambard Kingdom Brunel, was begun in 1836. By far the most delicate of the suspension bridges, it spanned 700 ft (210 m) with the lightness of wires, an engineering feat which has an effect on the onlooker quite as astounding as the first glimpse of a great medieval cathedral.

Iron was king. Iron's great strength in compression allowed slender columns; there need be no waste of material, and columns could be cast by the thousands. Unnecessary walls and partitions were eliminated by the frame – constructed of the columns and beams. No wonder manufacturers fell for the frame. While bridge engineering put cast iron on the map, the idea spread rapidly to factories and mills, even office blocks. Strength in compression together with firm lateral support allowed taller buildings, and economies in land and money. A factory built in Derby in 1793 had exposed columns and was six stories high. Particularly good examples still standing include a warehouse at Milford, Derbyshire (1793), and an iron-framed flax-spinning mill at Shrewsbury (1796).

THE PALM HOUSE AT KEW

"Turner took a piece of paper, folding it to make a crease in the middle, then, with a pen, quickly traced a vertical profile of one half of the intended house on one side of the crease; then, folding the other half of the paper on the inked part and, on opening it, there was a section of the whole length of the palm-house, as it was afterwards erected..." In this way, the Dublin engineer, Richard Turner, explained his idea for the design of the Palm House at Kew Gardens, London. While Decimus Burton was the architect the records suggest it was Turner's idea. The description fits a designer who had rapid visions of structure and form – which is precisely what the Palm House conveys.

The direct inspiration for the Palm House was, however, the Great Conservatory at Chatsworth House, Derbyshire, completed in 1840, and designed by the Duke of Devonshire's gardener Sir Joseph Paxton, with the assistance of Burton. The Palm House was begun in 1845 and completed in 1847; bigger than the Chatsworth conservatory, but smaller than the Crystal Palace built in 1851 and 1,851 ft (560 m) long, the Palm House is 106 ft (32 m) wide, 62 ft (19 m) high at the center, and 362 ft (109 m) long. Its form derives from roughly semi-circular ribs of cast iron.

At the center are two tiers of ribs, with the ends of the first tier supported on two lines of cast iron

The interior of Stanley Mill at Stroud in Gloucestershire (1813): mass production and an end to partitions

columns. At this level, lateral stability is achieved by a cast iron balcony which acts, in effect, as a ring beam which is, again, supported by the lines of columns. It is from this ring-beam balcony, supported at the ends by the semi-circular ribs and circular staircases (also in cast iron) that the second tier of ribs springs.

It is an ingeniously simple, functional structure where both form and detail reflect the shape and delicacy of palm leaves, and where every element – brackets, half-vaults (as in Gothic church design) and balcony – is performing an important job. Yet every piece from which the house is made was prefabricated, and, in some cases, such as the iron glazing divisions, run off by the thousand.

The conception of the building was complex; but once devised, it was simple to make. All the same, the organization of its manufacture was itself complex.

The Palm House, Kew Gardens, London

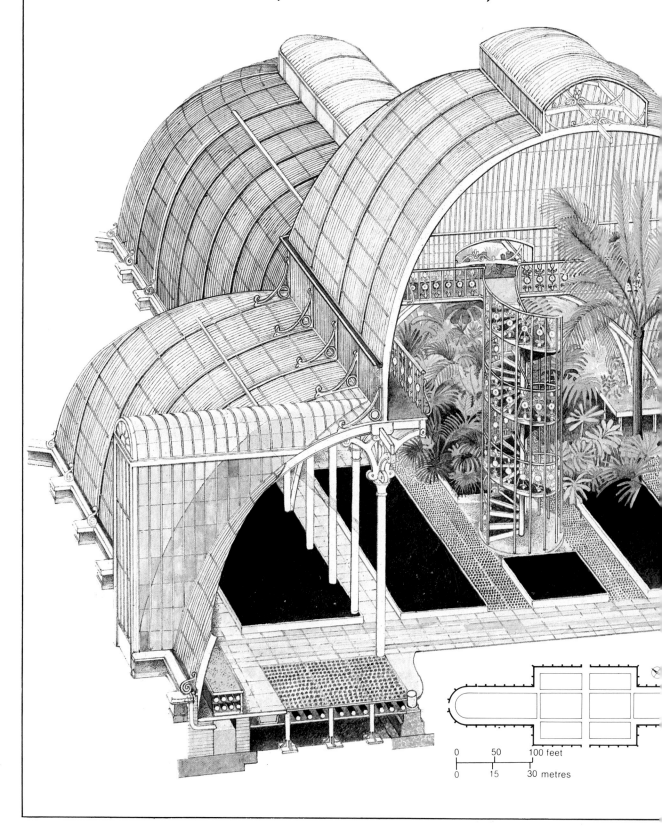

0	50	100 feet
0	15	30 metres

The cast iron parts, while treated decoratively with botanical themes, are all essential elements of the structure. They were all pre-cast in large numbers and brought to the site for assembly. The speed of conception and construction (the latter took two years, 1845–7) was quite unprecedented.

New methods of construction developed by engineers for bridges, technical developments in the production of cast iron, and later the introduction in the 1860s of Bessemer's process of steel production opened up possibilities of wider, taller buildings with a more flexible plan. The use of plate glass in quantity, and its substitution for walls, meant that these buildings were quick to assemble and would be well lit. The possibilities of covering large areas for hundreds of people introduced a new range of types of building, such as exhibition halls and shopping arcades. Among the better-known examples are the Galeries St Hubert in Brussels (1839–46), the Galleria Vittorio Emmanuele, Milan (1865–77), London's Crystal Palace (1851), and New York's (1852). In London it was possible to move the Crystal Palace, because of the new methods of construction, from Hyde Park to Sydenham in 1854.

The earlier pioneers in the use of iron and glass construction were the builders of railway sheds, that at Euston, London (1839) and Trijunct Station, Derby (1840), in particular. This mixed-construction approach was continued in such great termini as King's Cross (1851–2) and Paddington (1854). The use of iron and glass for buildings of established types was not at the time considered acceptable.

Kew Palm House illustrates clearly the challenge of the new engineering to architecture. It is above all a functional building, carefully designed to house exotic equatorial plants. The micro-climate is maintained by water (collected from the great glass roof) which is heated and then run through pipes (5½ miles of them) beneath the pierced cast iron floor.

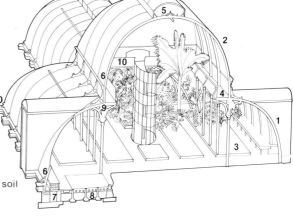

1   First tier of ribs
2   Second tier of ribs, semicircular
3   Pillars supporting the two tiers
4   Balcony acting as a ring-beam
5   Lantern (62 ft above ground level)
6   Gutters
7   Water tank
8   Heating pipes under the floor and soil
9, 10   Botanical motifs on structural elements

Charles Dickens pictures the difficulties in writing about the construction of the Crystal Palace: ". . . . the glass-maker promised to supply, in the required time nine hundred thousand square feet of glass . . . in separate panes, and these the largest that ever were made in sheet glass; each being forty-nine inches long. The iron-master passed his word in like manner to columns varying from fourteen-and-a-half to twenty feet in length; thirty-four miles of guttering tube, to join every individual tube together, under the ground; two thousand two hundred and twenty-four girders; besides eleven hundred and twenty-eight bearers for supporting galleries . . ."

Of course the Crystal Palace was far bigger than the Palm House, yet this gives some idea of how such a vast undertaking – the first all-glass public building – was put together.

Right: the western train shed at Liverpool Street Station in London, designed by Edward Wilson (1875)

Glass and iron were also being introduced to cover the fashionable new shopping arcades. Below right: the Galeries St Hubert in Brussels, by J. P. Cluysenaar (1839–46). Below left: the Old Arcade, Cleveland, Ohio, by Eisenmann and Smith (1890)

STYLE

The industrial style was part of a tremendous 19th-century drive which kept pace with technological advances, and which helped make canals, railways and an empire. Like the Roman style it was about expansion: empire-building made people think big – construction was on the march, design was simplified, haste demanded repetition. Architecture became functional, and detail superfluous except to embellish strong, plain forms – such as scrolls in brackets, plant themes in balustrades, and leafy capitals at iron column-heads.

The style was about trade, commerce, communications: hence bridges, viaducts, dockyards, factories, mills, railroad stations – structures and buildings which were needed quickly, and which were completely outside the aesthetic world of fashion and taste. The style is the product of a hard-headed world. Deriving its impetus from engineering, selecting relevant building-parts from material immediately available, the industrial style is the product of whatever machinery could manufacture. A tool was needed, and it was found in this style. Yet the embellishments were rich, and the forms arising from the daring structural systems were often noble. But these riches originated in parts that could be run off in the factory by the thousand, as we see from the structures of railway sheds, office buildings and, most dramatically of all, the Crystal Palace.

MACHINE-PRODUCED PARTS

Inspired, like the Crystal Palace, by the discovery of a new building material, all the great structural undertakings of the period required an unshakable act of faith in machine production. This faith kept design bristling with confidence and imagination. Not surprisingly, the style spread widely, encompassing the hundreds of details and necessities of life which enrich villages, towns and cities. All that could be was mass-produced – pillar-boxes, lettering-types, bollards, verandahs, balustrades, brackets, railings, staircases and banisters, light-fittings, streetlamp standards, city sculpture, reliefs, gates, gratings, manhole covers, urns and gutters.

To some contemporaries the boldness of the designs seemed brutal. But the style soon traveled widely because it was needed. It developed most quickly in the USA. Cast iron structures and facades appeared in Pennsylvania in the 1820s, in New York in the 1830s, and in the 1850s office blocks with cast iron frames were being built in New York and Philadelphia. In 1852 an almost exact copy of the Crystal Palace was built in New York for a World Fair; like the English original it burnt to the ground. In the 1850s, too, while

Cast iron commercial structures in (left) Philadelphia (Hoxie & Button, c. 1860) and (right) New York (James Bogardus, 1848)

the enormous cathedral-like arches of Paddington Station were going up in London (I.K. Brunel and W.D. Wyatt, completed 1854), the cast iron structures of Les Halles Centrales in Paris were begun, and the iron-framed Bibliothèque Ste-Geneviève in Paris in neo-Classical style (1843–50), and parts of the Bibliothèque Nationale (1862–8) with its traditional pendentived domes on cast iron columns, both by Henri Labrouste. Conservatories became fashionable in France, Poland and Russia, and the spirit of the conservatory inspired the design of covered markets and shopping arcades as far away as India, South Africa, Australia and Chile.

Oriel Chambers, Liverpool (Peter Ellis, 1864–5) has a cast iron frame; the Gothic masonry has little structural use

CHAPTER 17

Modern Movements

Above: Falling Water, Bear Run, Pennsylvania (1936), by Frank Lloyd Wright. Very low ceilings internally achieve the feeling of the massive weight of rock. The landscape is viewed through horizontal slits as if in strata

Below: Expo '70 Pavilion, Tokyo, by Powell and Moya. The roof hovers over a free arrangement of spaces below, where traditional Japanese under-eaves architecture is re-created in utterly modern manner

Three architects have had the greatest influence on the forms and appearance of 20th-century architecture – Le Corbusier, Frank Lloyd Wright and Mies van der Rohe. To these three we can trace the three distinct strands in modern design. There was the whitewashed style of the 1920s and 1930s, with a cubist look, horizontal windows, flat roofs, the precision of a machine aesthetic; there was the intermixing of landscape and living rooms, timber structures floating over dips of natural contours, huge spreading eaves, natural materials such as stone and cedar-wood boarding; and there was the glass house, transparent, constructed of polished steel, with the horizontals of floors and roofs heavily accentuated. All these characteristics can be traced back to these three architects.

Each man had his own followers through whom the movement spread. How many people realize, for instance, that sun-terraces, open-plans and roof gardens were invented by Le Corbusier; that boarded houses, "split levels," and the use of natural materials and ground slopes are inherited from Wright; and that Mies van der Rohe's two glass skyscrapers (in Chicago and New York) were copied by others, to be scattered across the skylines of the world's cities?

Between them, these architects have had an enormous, if indirect, influence on the appearance of the 20th century. In assessing the technological advances of the 19th century, they saw how steel and reinforced concrete could be put together as architecture. They inherited the structural developments of the Industrial Style, at once thrilling and difficult to handle. Wright, for instance, did not reject the machine; but it was partly his fear of its misuse which led him, at least at the beginning, to look to nature for inspiration. Le Corbusier, on the other hand, like Mies van der Rohe, was fascinated by technology, and he saw in it ways to solve 20th-century problems.

Le Corbusier loved cities; Wright hated them. But our architects agreed on one point: they were appalled to see new kinds of structure dressed up and smothered in the drab old-fashioned clothes of neo-Classical styles. Architects wanted to see new structures expressed honestly; they were beautiful in

Chrysler Tower, New York (1929), by W. van Allen. "Odeon" style with fins. The crowning glory of Manhattan skyscrapers is in the authentic all-American mold of the property boom

themselves. The obsolete clothes had to be stripped off; it was essential to get back to first principles, to start with a clean sheet.

In stripping designs of every kind of clutter, from traditional details to roomfuls of dusty furniture, architects found that forms and spaces were seen at their best and most sculptural in white. "White," Le Corbusier said, "is absolute." White gives the maximum light of reflection and thus the greatest appreciation of the extent of a space. White also links with the cubist movement in Paris, deriving from Cézanne and established by Gris, Picasso, Braque, and Léger. It is with the work of such painters that Le Corbusier's is inseparably linked.

LE CORBUSIER

For the background of contemporary architecture – the cubist whiteness which took such a hold before World War II, and the rough concrete buildings with flat tops and sides which have dominated the post-war period – one returns to Le Corbusier as the chief source of inspiration, albeit often misused and misunderstood.

When Le Corbusier arrived in Paris and set up an office just after World War I, there was no European architectural movement. There were just a few isolated modern buildings by architects such as Adolf Loos (who introduced Le Corbusier to concrete) and Peter Behrens (for whom Le Corbusier worked); and in 1919, the year before Le Corbusier settled in Paris, Walter Gropius launched the Bauhaus school of industrial and architectural design in Germany. All these were beginnings that had as yet no direction. Le Corbusier gave the style direction. When he made the remark "a house is a machine for living in" he meant simply that the building must work, as anything from a painting to a car must work. At another level, however, he was regarding a house as he might regard a machine; the parts have no meaning on their own, but when they are put together they work together to achieve more than the sum of the parts. In the same way, rooms in a house have no meaning when separate, yet as parts of a more important whole (the architectural form) they work together to make a beautiful place to live in.

As Brunelleschi and Alberti went back to the Romans for guidance, so Le Corbusier went back to the ancient Greeks, and was the only architect of his time to do so. At the same time, technological advances supplied both the means to solve modern problems and the opportunity to free space from the imprisoning grip of the load-bearing walls of traditional structures. Add Le Corbusier's passion for cubist forms – the cube itself, the pyramid, the cone, the cylinder – and his exposure of these whitewashed shapes to light and shade, and you have the principal parts he put together to create the modern style.

CONCRETE AND CUBISM

Le Corbusier fell in love with reinforced concrete because its structural frame freed space in the way that the Greek column and beam had previously done. His ambition to purify architecture led to his love of white, the bond between his early buildings, and between the various movements of the 1920s and 1930s: the white style of architecture became famous. The work of his cubist decade included Maison la Roche, Paris (1922–4), the Villa Stein, Garches (1927), the Villa Savoye, Poissy (1929–31), and the Pavilion Suisse, Paris (1931–2). The innovations in these buildings sparked the imagination of architects: the columns carrying the building (pilotis), the sun terrace (on the flat roof), the open plan, glass walls, the cantilever and the rediscovery of Classical proportion.

Le Corbusier's ideas were widely copied. Important examples of his influence are the Schröder House,

Highpoint, Highgate, by Berthold Lubetkin. With this and other buildings Lubetkin established the modern architectural movement in London

Utrecht (1924) by Rietveld, the Highpoint Flats, London (1933–5) by Lubetkin, the Library at Viipuri (1927–35) by Aalto, and the Doldertal Apartments, Zurich (1936) by Breuer and Roth. The architecture of these remarkable designers influenced European students in the 1930s, transforming Le Corbusier's handful of disciples into a following of thousands.

FRANK LLOYD WRIGHT

By the 1930s modern architecture was already firmly established in the United States. Over the last 30 years Frank Lloyd Wright had completed a number of great works. Brought up on the land, Wright drew inspiration from natural forms – he believed architecture should balance with these forms.

The nearest available model was the Oriental house; and Wright was much influenced by the philosophy lying behind traditional Japanese domestic architecture. Japanese sympathy with nature, the Japanese house's huge roof and open plan, and the plan's relatedness to the garden, coincided with Wright's vision of a new architecture in the tradition of the log cabin.

Wright saw architecture as shelter; this is why he stressed the roof, the podium (security in foundations) and the fireplace. Like European architects, he stressed the essentials of living; but essentials that were bound up with the American pioneering spirit, the need for security in a great space. The chief characteristics of his work stayed with him throughout his life, and were established early at the D. D. Martin House, Buffalo (1904), and the famous Robie House,

Chicago (1908–9). Both these reveal a passionate interest in structure based on traditional materials – wood, brick, stone – and the forms which followed. The focus of the structure in his houses was almost always the enormous fireplace; but the cantilevers he achieved with wooden roof trusses were breathtaking. The roofs and overhanging eaves provided a giant frame beneath which the plan of the building could freely evolve to make its connections with the garden and landscape, through the light windows and the terraces along the huge podiums. Thus we have a magnificent build-up of walls to terraces to windows to roofs – culminating in a great chimney, the ancient symbol of the hearth, warmth and survival.

THE COMING OF GLASS AND STEEL

Wright's architecture began to change in the 1930s, influenced by European architects fleeing from Nazism – Mies van der Rohe, Breuer, Gropius and many others went to America. It was largely through van der Rohe's glass and steel architecture for the Illinois Institute of Technology (plan 1940, built c. 1942–56), his Chicago skyscrapers (1948–51) and the Seagram Building in New York (1958) that a EuroAmerican glass-and-steel style grew up on the American East coast, helping to create the European tower-block style of the 1960s.

Reinforced concrete emerges as the structural material dominating 20th-century architecture. For the first time since the Romans, concrete was developed as

Seagram Building, New York (1958), by Mies van der Rohe. This elegant style depended on minute attention to the design of detail

a structural material in the 1870s. The combination of concrete and steel created a material that was cheap, strong in compression and tension, and easy and quick to make. Wooden shuttering is constructed by carpenters in the form of a beam or column, into which is poured a mix of cement, sand, crushed brick or pebbles and water, to surround a network of steel rods, placed at the lower half of the beam and in the center section of the column. Once made, the shuttering can be reused to prefabricate further columns and beams. Precast or made *in situ* reinforced concrete slabs span between beams to form floors and panels of light materials such as glass or wood often fill the space between columns.

Much quicker to build and stronger than brickwork, concrete withstands heat and flame-spread in a way that steel does not.

THE CORBUSIER CENTER, ZURICH

Le Corbusier tried everything. He invented structures, explored all possible forms and materials, worked in concrete, steel and glass, moved to stone and brick, and returned to concrete again. His total oeuvre was a kind of recapitulation of Classical architecture – he stepped out from the Parthenon, drew inspiration from the Renaissance, worked through Baroque and, at the end, returned to the ancient Greek model using steel and glass. He was like, as he once remarked, an echo of past civilizations; if the Unité d'Habitation at Marseilles (1947–52) was Classical in conception, the Notre Dame du Haut, Ronchamp (1950–5) was Baroque. Then, in 1963, came his model based on the final plans for the Corbusier Center, Zurich. It contained many of his favorite ideas. Beneath an independent triangulated roof was a building with its own roof and an irregular plan derived from two small concrete cubes, divided by a ramp. One cube was solid, the other open-work, with random window divisions.

But if you walk across the smooth lawn of the City Park, Zurich, you find a structure of intensely bright colors made entirely of steel, glass, and enameled panels. The magician has worked his last trick; apart from the ramp the concrete has vanished. But the idea is as before, two cubes each subdivided into four square spaces under a lightly supported cover. It is a stunning building; it seems to be as much a culmination of 20th-century architecture as the conclusion of the influences, inventions, and ideas of a lifetime. The Greek temple, the cube and the glass-and-steel of the 1920s, the roof garden, and his last geometric paintings seem to come together, suddenly, in a multicolored blaze.

Totally free-form, Corbusier's masterly Ronchamp Chapel seems to take off from the crest of the hill like a ship in full sail

The Corbusier Center is a setting for the architecture, paintings, sculpture, and writings of its maker: a place where people can meet and talk, cook a meal, have informal discussions, and show the work of other artists. The whole structure, according to Le Corbusier, is designed in terms of display: the triangulated roof is "the architecture," the independent construction below is an exhibition pavilion for his paintings and sculpture. This pavilion was, however, designed as a house, since only a house has the right scale for the paintings and sculpture to be seen in. Only in this way could he combat the remoteness and distant solemnity of the usual museum.

So Le Corbusier designed a "house" on two floors, with a kitchen, circular stair, a ramp, and a roof terrace. Ceilings, regulated by Le Corbusier's Modular system dimensions, are only 7 ft 6 in (2.3 m) high. The "house" is small – overall, it is hardly more than 15 ft (4.6 m) high. Art must relate to people, and people must relate to their surroundings; but these surroundings must also relate to the outside world – in this case the park. Hence the roof structure – the architectural frame, linking the exterior with the interior, the scale of the park with the scale of the "house," very much as the peristyle does in an ancient Greek temple. Inside the Center you really feel you are in a house. There is the kitchen; a bathroom and bedrooms could be easily added with the help of a few screens. A blue ramp takes you to the first floor, from which a circular stair leads to the terrace above which the great structure dips down over you.

This is the climax of the building. You can walk about on the roof, just below the red, white, and green triangles which frame the park and make more green triangles. So from the shelter of the roof you feel part of the park. Nature and the platform under the roof merge. From the pressed steel seats, flowing round in

Le Corbusier Center, Zurich

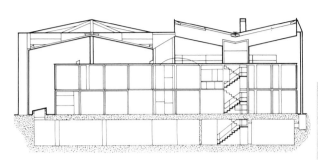

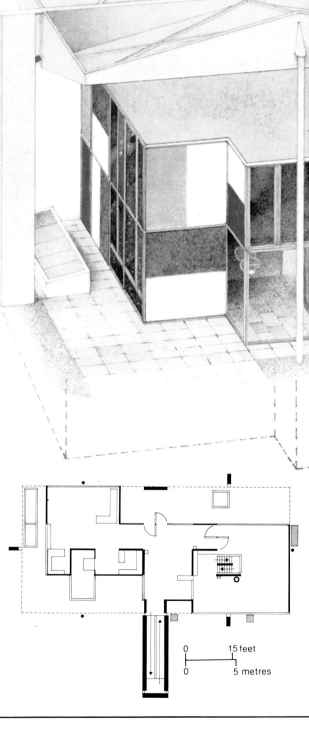

Le Corbusier (Charles Édouard Jeanneret) (1889–1973) not only built, he wrote polemics on architecture. In Towards a New Architecture (1923) he set out the principles underlying his work – at that time the white houses of his "cubist" decade. "The plan holds in itself the essence of sensation," he wrote. Planning includes setting the building in relation to others and to the landscape or garden that surrounds and may even invade it. The exterior of the building is the result of the interior plan. Among his "five points of a new architecture" were: columns (pilotis) supporting the building; free ("open") plan; flat roof with garden; the long window; the free facade supported on cantilevers. His respect for Classical order led to the design of a Modular system of dimensions based on the human figure.

The Le Corbusier Center in Zurich City Park was designed by the architect in 1963 to display his own paintings and sculpture. It contains many of his favorite ideas. Beneath the triangulated roof, from the roof garden, as through the windows below, architecture and landscape are brought together. The "double-cube" forms (one solid, one open-work) of the "home" below are quite small (15ft high), based on Modular dimensions (see the cross-section and plan). The brightly colored whole is made of glass, steel, and enameled panels – the concrete restricted to the pilotis and the ramp linking the two "cubes." This stunning building seems as much a culmination of 20th-century architecture as of the ideas of one architect's lifetime.

0	15 feet
0	5 metres

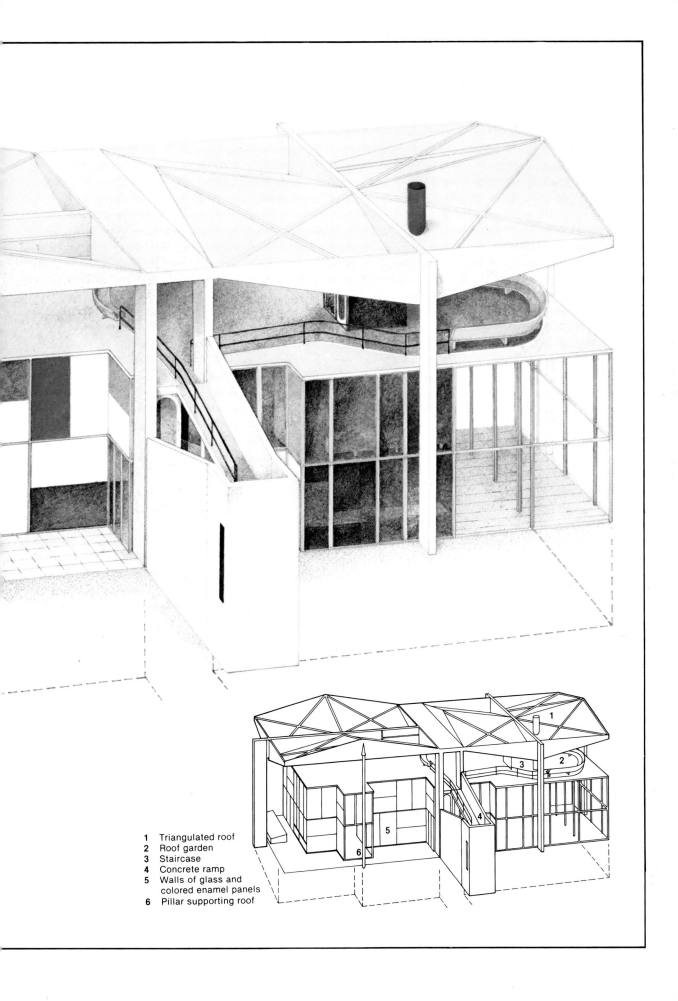

1 Triangulated roof
2 Roof garden
3 Staircase
4 Concrete ramp
5 Walls of glass and
  colored enamel panels
6 Pillar supporting roof

a free-hand line, you can sit and admire the trees and the sky in your private roof-garden. You discover that the frame and the "house" are part of each other, as they are of the park. Now you begin to understand the Corbusier Center. All the parts of it – the spaces outside, the people and the paintings, and the objects which inhabit it – are part of the same picture. As you look back across the park you see this picture by Le Corbusier as yet another double-image. In one, you discover the proportions which relate to people, and so to the spaces inside, of which the shapes outside are an exact description. In the next, you discover that the building suggests a temple where the frame shades the detail of the geometric mosaic from the glare of the sun.

WILLIAM MORRIS AND THE MODERN AGE

Architects of the 20th century looked back at extraordinary developments in technology and saw what could be made of them in terms of architecture. Le Corbusier used this technology, for example, to lay out a capital city at Chandigarh in the Punjab (1950–65) to match the background scale of the Himalayas. Similarly Jørn Utzon used modern technology in his design for the Sydney Opera House (1975); and Alvar Aalto to create a single vast space at his concert hall in Helsinki (1970).

Yet engineering is only part of the story of modern architecture. Another contributor to the modern movement was a 19th-century Englishman, William Morris. Morris is one of history's household names for his superb wallpaper and textile designs. But Morris hated the machine; it destroyed quality, it eliminated the craftsman, men were deprived of the pleasure of making things with their own hands, and of communicating this pleasure to the article made. This was true whether the article was a building, a textile, or a piece of furniture. Morris regarded the revivalists as plainly mad; the arguments should not be about what style to pin to the facade of a civic hall or bank, but about what kind of design suits the purpose.

As for crafts, Morris's rejection of the machine and insistence on quality led him and his followers to make furniture, wallpapers and textiles with their own hands, dreaming of an ideal world where everyone could buy honest, well-designed, well-made articles. But Morris refused to accept the machine and his vision led nowhere. Only the reduction in costs made possible by standardization put articles within the reach of most people; yet the machine destroyed both quality and flexibility.

What a prophet! Morris realized that the machine denied the rights of the individual. If, on the one hand, the movement led to the affectation of Art

Utzon's spectacular Opera House (1975) shares dominance of Sydney Harbor with the Harbor Bridge (1932). Opera house, concert hall (behind) and restaurant, each has its own curved concrete vaults

Finlandia Hall, Helsinki (1970), by Alvar Aalto. The glacial calm of white marble, the winged balconies of the dark blue interior, could belong to nowhere but Finland

Above: Kuwait Water Towers (1978), by Lindström, Egnell and Björn. One of five groups around Kuwait city, these structures take their inspiration from the oasis: palm trees round water

Below: Guggenheim Museum, New York (1959), by Frank Lloyd Wright. The entire exhibition is displayed on a circular ramp: thus the aimlessness of the run-of-the-mill museum is eliminated

Nouveau, it also led to the Werkbund in Sweden in 1910, the Design and Industries Association in England in 1915, and, through art and architectural schools adopting design into the curricula, to Gropius's Bauhaus, and, most recently, to Habitat in Britain.

At the same time, Morris's ideas led on to an architecture of individual minds – to Philip Webb, Charles Voysey, Charles Rennie Mackintosh, Louis Sullivan, Frank Lloyd Wright, Walter Gropius and Le Corbusier, and to their followers – for example Aalto in Finland, Arne Jacobsen and Utzon in Denmark, and Goff in America. For however much modern architecture is influenced by mechanization, it is still the individual artist and craftsman who determines the style. Conversely, the misuse of the machine has destroyed the hopes of modern architects, for the responsibility for design has been shifted from the architect to such methods as industrialized building systems of prefabrication which exclude the individual contribution of artist and craftsman. The constructions

that result are profoundly unsatisfactory because building systems are static, incapable of change or adapting to human variations and preferences. Hence identical tower blocks: the machine makes tall buildings easy.

And so modern architecture is largely a matter of isolated buildings or building schemes in various parts of the world. Often gems of design, these works and their architects have had an influence on general standards. From its inception the modern style spread rapidly, helped by modern communications: Holland (Stijl movement), 1920s; Switzerland (Maillart), 1920s; Sweden (Asplund) and Finland (Aalto), late 1920s; England (Lubetkin), early 1930s; Italy (Nervi), early 1930s; and Brazil (Niemeyer), middle 1930s.

Above: European Investment Bank, Luxemburg (1981), by Denys Lasdun, Redhouse and Softley. High-security entry is achieved with visual sleight of hand

Below: Hyatt Regency Hotel, Atlanta (1974), by John Portman. Portman invented the now-fashionable many-tiered "atrium"

Left: St Columbus School extension, Dublin, by Scott, Tallon and Walker. A delicate glass-cage structure stepping lightly over the ground

Below: Communist Party HQ, Paris (1980), by Oscar Niemeyer. Above the underground offices, all is daylight. Even the corridor curves away and evaporates through light screens, like transparencies

125

Glossary

Agora *Greek equivalent of the Roman forum.*
Aisle *Division parallel with the nave in a church.*
Arabesque *Light surface detail often used by Arabian artists.*
Arcade *Group of arches on columns or pillars.*
Atrium *Important apartment in Roman house; court or entrance hall, with an open roof in the center and pool below.*
Baldacchino *Canopy supported by columns, usually over an altar or tomb.*
Balustrade *Series of pillars or columns supporting a handrail or coping.*
Basilica *Church with aisles and a nave higher than the aisles.*
Buttress *Masonry built against a wall to resist the pressure of a vault or arch.*
Cantilever *Horizontal projection supported by downward force behind a fulcrum.*
Caryatid *Sculptured figure used as a support.*
Cladding *Outer veneer of various materials.*
Clerestory *Upper part of church nave, with windows above aisle roofs.*
Coffer *Sunk panel in ceiling, vault or dome.*
Colonnade *Range of columns.*
Cornice *Projecting top of an entablature, or projecting top course of any building.*
Crossing *Intersection of nave, transept and chancel.*
Drum *Circular or polygonal structure raising a dome.*
Entablature *Horizontal top part of a Classical order.*
Fluting *Vertical channeling in column.*
Forum *Central market and meeting place in Roman towns.*
Fresco *Originally wall painting applied on wet plaster; any non-oil based wall painting.*
Frieze *Middle part of entablature.*
Greek Cross *Cross with four arms of equal length.*
Lintel *Horizontal timber or stone spanning an opening.*
Megaron *Principal room of Aegean house.*
Mullion *Vertical division of a window.*
Nave *Western arm or central aisle of church.*
Pedestal *Support for a column, statue or vase.*
Pediment *Triangular or segmental upright front end of moderately-pitched roof.*
Pendentive *Vaulting device for roofing a square plan with a circular dome.*
Peristyle *Range of columns surrounding a court or temple.*
Pier *Mass of masonry from which an arch springs.*
Pilaster *A pillar-shaped projection in a wall.*
Pilotis *Posts on an unenclosed ground floor supporting a raised building.*
Plinth *Projecting base of a building or column.*
Podium *Continuous pedestal.*
Portico *Colonnaded arch forming a vestibule or entrance, with a roof supported by columns.*
Rib *Projecting band on a ceiling or vault.*
Rotonda *Round building.*
Stucco *Fine quality of plaster, used for low relief work and external surfaces.*
Stupa *Mound forming Buddhist sacred monument.*
Tie-bar *Beam, rod or bar tying parts of a building together.*
Triforium *Space between sloping roof and vaulting of church aisle.*
Triglyph *Vertical grooved member of Doric frieze.*
Truss *Number of timbers framed together to bridge a span or form a bracket.*
Vault *Arched covering in stone or brick.*
Voussoir *Wedge-shaped block forming part of the arch of a door or window.*

Further Reading

Sir Banister Fletcher, *History of Architecture*, (R.I.B.A., London; rev. edn. 1975).

Lord Clark, *Civilisation* (B.B.C./John Murray, London, 1969).

Christian Norberg-Schulz, *Meaning in Western Architecture* (Studio Vista, 1975).

V. Gordon Childe, *New Light on the Most Ancient East* (Routledge, London, 1958).

Werner Blaser, *Structure and Form in Japan* (Verlag für Architektur, Zurich).

Sir Nikolaus Pevsner, *An Outline of European Architecture* (Penguin, London, 1970).

Nelson Wu, *Chinese and Indian Architecture* (Studio Vista, London, 1968).

Sir John Summerson, *Georgian London* (Barrie and Jenkins, London, 1970).

Vincent Scully, *American Architecture and Urbanism* (Thames and Hudson, London, 1969).

Rene Huyghe (ed.), *Larousse Encyclopedia of Renaissance and Baroque Art* (Hamlyn, London, 1964).

Acknowledgments

Alinari, Florence: 62*tr*. Architectural Press, London: 118*t*. Graham Bateman, Oxford: 113*br*. Bildarchiv Foto Marburg, Marburg/Lahn: 50, 51*t*, 51*b*, 52*tr*, 60*tr*, 63*tr*, 70*b*, 103*t*. Brecht-Einzig, London: 122*br*. John Brennan, Oxford: 92, 119. Casa Editrice Scoda, Milan: 62*br*. Ian Cook, London: 123*t*. Le Corbusier Centre, Zurich: 120. Design Aspects, London: 68*b*, 108*t*, 117. Douglas Dickens, London: 97*b*, 101*bl*, 102*br*, 102*bl*. Elsevier, Amsterdam: 32*t*. Robert Estall, London: 110*tr*. Werner Forman, London: 40*b*, 41*t*, 85. Fotique, Bath: 90*tl*. Fototeca Unione, Rome: 25. Mario Gerardi, Rome: 22*bl*, 23*b*, 27*t*, 27*br*. Giraudon, Paris: 47*tr*. Tim Graham, London: 111, 113*tr*. Sonia Halliday, Weston Turville: 9*b*, 13, 29*t*, 30*t*, 30*b*, 38*b*, 48*t*, 52*bl*, 54*bl*, 56*tl*, 56*br*, 62*bl*, 80*bl*. Robert Harding, London: frontispiece, 8, 16, 53, 72*b*, 74*bl*, 76, 77*bl*, 81*t*, 88*b*, 95*b*, 100. John Hillelson, London: 11. Michael Holford, Loughton: 10*br*, 10*bl*, 26, 42*r*, 45*br*, 58*tr*, 58*bl*, 59*b*, 60*bl*, 86, 89*tl*. Holle, Baden-Baden: 45*bl*. Alan Hutchison, London: 42*l*, 79, 81*bl*, 82*b*, 83*bl*, 83*cb*, 83*cc*, 101*t*, 101*br*. Institute of Archaeology, University of London: 10*t* (photo R.A.F. © reserved). Jarrold, Norwich: 105*br*. A.F. Kersting, London: 39, 54*tr*, 69, 74*cl*, 75*tl*, 75*cl*, 75*tr*, 77*tr*, 80*tl*, 90*bl*, 91*tr*, 91*br*, 96*b*, 96*t*, 106*t*, 106*b*, 110*tl*, 110*c*, 115*b*. Denys Lasdun Redhouse & Softley, London: 124*t*. Andrew Lawson, Charlbury: 95*t*. Ben Lenthall, Oxford: 124*b*. Oscar Niemeyer, Paris: 125*b* (photo M. Moch). Observer Colour Magazine, London: 125*t*. Oronoz, Madrid: 34, 36. Powell & Moya, London: 116*b*. Mike Roberts Color Productions, Berkley, Ca.: 98. Ann Ronan, London: 109. Scala, Florence: 17*br*, 19, 24*bl*, 27*bl*, 32*b*, 33*tr*, 46, 47*tl*, 48*b*, 52*tl*, 59*t*, 62*tl*, 63*bl*, 64*tl*, 64*br*, 65, 66, 67*b*, 67*t*, 68*cl*, 70*t*, 73*tr*, 74*tl*. Edwin Smith, Saffron Walden: 32*t*. Spectrum, London: 17*t*, 37. Ed Teitelman, New Jersey: 107, 114*bl*, 114*br*, 115*tl*, 115*tr*, 116*t*. Vision International, London: 114*tr*. Stuart Windsor, London: 123*b*. Zefa, London: 9*tr*, 15, 17*bl*, 20*t*, 20*b*, 21*t*, 29*b*, 33*tl*, 33*b*, 35*t*, 35*bl*, 35*br*, 38*t*, 40*t*, 41*b*, 45*t*, 60*tl*, 78, 81*c*, 82*t*, 83*t*, 84*t*, 88*t*, 88*b*, 89*tr*, 97*t*, 102*t*, 103*b*, 108*c*, 108*b*, 118*b*, 122*bl*.

The Publishers have attempted to observe the legal requirements with respect to the rights of the suppliers of photographic materials. Nevertheless, persons who have claims are invited to apply to the Publishers.

Artwork: color by Dick Barnard and Graham Smith; line by John Brennan.

Index